Dream Class

JME Publishing

San Diego, California

smartclassroommanagement.com

Printed in the U.S.A.

Many thanks to:

Kathleen Chappel

Mike McKown

Lucy Goodwin

Mike Welch

Diane Lueke

I.S.B.N. 978-1889236-33-9

Dream Class

How To Transform *Any* Group
Of Students Into The Class
You've Always Wanted

MICHAEL LINSIN

Contents

The heart is a bloom.

—U2, "Beautiful Day"

Preface

British explorer Earnest Shackleton is widely considered one of the greatest leaders of the 20th Century. While attempting to cross the Antarctic in 1914, his expedition ship, Endurance, became trapped and eventually crushed by the pressure of ten million tons of ice, leaving his crew stranded on the frozen pack of the Weddell Sea. Shortly afterward, Shackleton and his crew marched across the shifting ice field until reaching water. There, they set out in three small lifeboats in search of safety. After seven days, they landed on the rocky shores of uninhabited Elephant Island.

Nearly a year later, and after suffering through bitter cold and the threat of death and starvation, all 27 crew members were rescued by Shackleton himself, who had set out with five others three and a half months earlier aboard one of the lifeboats in search of South Georgia Island and the whaling station located there. Their 17-day voyage over some of the roughest waters in the world is now considered one of the greatest nautical crossings ever completed. Upon reaching South Georgia Island, Shackleton and two others hiked over mountains and across glaciers to reach the whaling station sheltered on the opposite side of the island.

It was a remarkable achievement, and Shackleton was hailed a hero. His ability to keep morale high and motivate his crew to work together throughout brutally trying circumstances is regarded as the ultimate example of leadership. The decisions Shackleton made, from organizing competitive football games on the ice to serving hot milk to his crew in the early mornings, were done to build trust, raise spirits, and promote togetherness. By all accounts, he transformed them into an outstanding crew, even a dream crew.

> *Like many new teachers, the only experience I had in such an environment was driving by on the freeway.*

Shackleton took a group of individuals from all walks of life—scientists, doctors, cooks, deckhands, and even a stowaway—and turned them into a compassionate, highly-motivated team, able to work side by side to overcome seemingly insurmountable odds to survive.

I read about Shackleton's historic adventure many years ago while studying to become a teacher. After earning my credential, I accepted a position teaching fourth grade in an inner-city school. The neighborhood surrounding the school was plagued with gangs, drugs, and poverty. Like many new teachers, the only experience I had in such an environment was driving by on the freeway. But Shackleton's story illustrated for me that with the right leadership skills one could not only persevere in the midst of difficult circumstances but thrive in spite of them.

The ideas explained in this book are the culmination of 20 years of actively searching for, identifying, and then implementing those critical elements that make the greatest difference in the classroom. By following them, the goal is not for you to simply improve, but to become an extraordinary teacher.

Effective teaching is more about *how* you teach your students—your interactions and relationships with them and the climate you create—and is less about what tools you use to teach them. Curriculum planning and management procedures are important, but they're not difference makers. In fact, two teachers using the same curriculum and materials and enforcing the same set of rules can experience vastly different levels of success with their students.

In this book, you will learn about the difference makers. Presented in the form of 15 keys, you will learn how to take any group of students and transform them into the class you envisioned when you first decided to become a teacher: your dream class.

It is my firm belief that no one should have to suffer through a stressful teaching environment or put up with students who are disrespectful, ill behaved, or uninterested. My hope is that this book will help you eliminate these frustrations and create, in their place, a dream class.

By the way:

The ideas presented in this book are based entirely upon my experiences as a classroom teacher. The stories I share are true. Only the names have been changed and some settings disguised to protect the innocent. (Or guilty, as the case may be.)

Dream Class

Allow Freedom Within Boundaries

Show Them How

Build Rapport

Give Worthy Praise

Cultivate Independence

Transform Limiting Beliefs

Take Responsibility

Hold Students Accountable

Be A Great Storyteller

Help Shy Students Flourish

Treat The Cause, Not The Symptoms

Involve And Utilize Parents

Develop Maturity

Free Your Room, Free Your Mind

See The Best In Your Students

One Last Thing

*What I dream of
is an art of balance.*

—*Henri Matisse*

Key #1

Allow Freedom Within Boundaries

I lost my way academically during middle school, and I have no one to blame but myself. I was a knucklehead, no doubt about it. I was so caught up in my budding social life that I couldn't be bothered with school. I flew under the radar of my parents and teachers, doing just enough to get by. In retrospect, it's hard for me to reconcile my middling efforts at the time with my current work ethic, but to my teenage-addled brain it seemed perfectly acceptable.

So I found myself entering high school unprepared for the increased rigor and far behind many of my classmates. Uninspired and lacking confidence, I slogged through the first semester of my freshman year earning mostly C's and D's. I hid in the back of the classroom and eked by only because I was a capable reader. Fate intervened in the second semester when I was placed in an English class taught by Bill Heyde.

A Gifted Teacher Makes All The Difference

Bill had a great personality—expressive and animated. I can remember the first time I sat in his classroom. I was initially taken aback by his off-the-chart passion and enthusiasm for English grammar, but I was quickly drawn in by his methods. I had never encountered a teacher like him before. He kidded and laughed with students regularly and loved to play practical jokes, but he was somehow able to keep a laser-like focus on his lesson objectives.

Bill became the academic lifeline I desperately needed, and I hung on for four years, taking a course from him every semester until I graduated.

Bill needled me right away, and I loved it. His class was fun, and for the first time since elementary school, I became genuinely interested in learning. Midway through the semester, he pulled me aside to tell me I was smart and capable of performing at a much higher level. It was a simple statement, but one laced with a not-so-subtle underlying challenge. It was also one of the best things anyone had ever said to me. Coming from someone I respected and admired, it had a powerful effect. I didn't want to let him down or prove him wrong, so I worked hard to excel.

Bill became the academic lifeline I desperately needed, and I hung on for four years, taking a course from him every semester until I graduated. I suffered occasional periods of doubt in my abilities, but Bill would have none of it. His near-constant encouragement and demand for hard work gave me the confidence to push through those challenging moments and come out the other side with the skills I needed to compete in college and beyond.

Privilege And Responsibility

Although there was plenty of good-natured banter between Bill and his students, he was mindful about treating each one with a certain scholarly respect. When they offered answers or opinions, Bill had a gift for making them feel as if their thoughts had genuine weight and relevance. He made his students feel like they were his intellectual equals having respectful discourse. This felt great, and it was a privilege being in his class. But with it came responsibility. There were boundaries that could never be crossed.

A Lesson Learned

Sitting in class one day, I was struck with an uncontrollable case of the giggles. A good friend was sitting across from me as we listened to Bill give directions for an assignment. Every time we made eye contact with each other, we broke up. This went on for a couple of minutes before Bill gave a quick glance, communicating that we should take care of it. We got quiet momentarily, but then made the mistake of looking at each other once again.

> *Upon hearing our muffled laughter, Bill said simply, "Get out."*

Upon hearing our muffled laughter, Bill said simply, "Get out." Looking surprised, we both immediately apologized and promised to stop. His response was the same, "Get out. I don't want you part of this class." He stood there silent and unmoving until we got up, collected our books, and left. A chill ran down my spine as I walked out of the room. He didn't tell us where to go or what to do.

The incident had such an impact on me that nearly 25 years later I can still remember it vividly. As I sat by myself in the student lounge, waiting out the hour, I was equal parts ashamed that I let him down and fearful that he wouldn't forgive me.

After school I immediately went to his office and apologized. He plainly wasn't happy with me. He didn't greet me with his usual smile and "Yo, Linsin!" He looked me squarely in the eye and said, "Don't let it happen again." That was it. There was no lecture, no arguing on my part, and no negotiation. Nothing else needed to be said. Implicit in his statement was that if it happened again, there would be a heavy consequence. How did I know this? Because I knew that Bill would never allow *any* student to interfere with the learning of others. I would come to learn that all great teachers share this trait.

> *It was a balancing act that few teachers achieve, but one in which students thrive.*

The next day, I was a nervous about going to his class. Would he treat me differently? My fears were quickly dispelled when he made a joke about it as soon as I walked in. It was his way of letting me know that all was forgiven. Exceptional teachers like Bill never hold a grudge against their students. In their eyes, every day is a new day. Despite my occasional transgressions, Bill continued to work with me until I graduated.

A Balance Of Opposites

I often sat at Bill's dining room table on Saturdays with a few other special "projects" as we wrote and revised our essays over and over again. He demanded hard work, but there was always an element of fun included. He was tough in the sense that he expected more out of his students than any other teacher, and as I experienced firsthand, there were boundaries that could never be crossed. But within those boundaries there was freedom to express oneself. It was a balancing act that few teachers achieve, but one in which students thrive. Those four years with him shaped not only my academic future but also the teacher I wanted to become.

Great teachers like Bill Heyde possess a balance of opposites that has always held fascination for me. The first week of my freshman year of college, I joined a Japanese karate club and started taking lessons. The style of karate I learned is called *Okinawan Goju-Ryu*. Goju-Ryu means hard and soft, and the dichotomy of these two opposites is intertwined throughout this ancient art. The notions of hard and soft mean much more than their literal interpretations.

The harmony between these two extremes is what makes the practice of this martial art effective, even nearly perfect. The strikes and kicks are hard and aggressive and are delivered with maximum power. At the other extreme, the blocks and defensive maneuvers are soft and supple, are executed in a slight retreat, and use the attacker's momentum as an advantage. Goju-Ryu's philosophy of self-defense is one of avoidance at all costs (soft) until attacked. Then it's 100% explosive power and commitment to defeating one's opponent (hard). Its movements are at once both beautiful (soft) and devastating (hard).

This balance of contrasts is a recurring theme among the most gifted teachers, those who make a lifelong impact on their students. The qualities of soft and hard in Goju-Ryu represent in great teachers their ability to balance freedom with boundaries.

A Model Teacher At Work

Recently, I was watching a veteran second-grade teacher teach a physical education lesson. It occurred to me while watching her that the lesson itself was a microcosm of an effective teacher's ability to embody these opposing ideas. The game they were playing was a simple one of four square. It's a game the students were already familiar with, yet the teacher didn't make assumptions.

She went over her expectations of behavior and reminded her class of the consequences if rules weren't followed. Next, she gave a detailed description of the rules of the game and modeled specific examples. She then had a few students play a mock game so that the other students could observe. She allowed for questions and made sure everyone understood what was expected of them. She was firm and exacting in setting up her boundaries for the game.

As the children played the game, the teacher smiled and laughed along with them but said little. She didn't micromanage because she didn't have to. She had been clear in her expectations, and her students knew what that meant. She just watched and enjoyed seeing them play in cooperation with one another. Once they began playing, she didn't add any additional expectations. She merely allowed them to play and express themselves within the boundaries given. These boundaries allowed the students the freedom to be themselves. Because they knew exactly where the line was, they could let down their guard and really have fun.

> *The message was clear. Have fun within the boundaries of my rules and expectations. Cross these boundary lines and you will not be allowed to participate.*

After several minutes, and much to the delight of her students, the teacher joined in. She looked like she was having as much fun as her class. She was laughing and playing with great enthusiasm, modeling and reinforcing acceptable, even expected, behavior. At one point, while waiting in line, a boy shoved another boy who he perceived was cutting in front of him. Immediately, the teacher stopped the game and removed the boy. In front of the class, she told him that his behavior was unacceptable and placed him in time-out.

The message was clear. Have fun within the boundaries of my rules and expectations. Cross these boundary lines and you will not be allowed to participate. Being part of our class is an honor and privilege, but with it comes responsibility and a high level of expectation. Fulfill the expectations and be a member of a special group. Otherwise, you're excluded. No exceptions.

Freedom And Boundaries

Like the aforementioned teacher, exceptional teachers guard and protect the sanctity of their classrooms by setting boundary lines of expected behavior and then enforcing them 100% of the time. These boundaries are non-negotiable, fixed, and rooted in the understanding that students who step outside of them interfere with learning. Within them, teachers are free to be inspiring, creative, and fun without the interruptions that mark less effective teachers. The students, knowing exactly where the boundary lines are, have the freedom to develop and excel without worrying whether another student is going to infringe upon their right to learn.

Boundaries, in the form of clearly defined rules and their consequences, are the foundation upon which inspired learning takes place. Without them, nothing will work as it should—or could. Far too many teachers believe that they possess them, but in fact have vague or movable boundary lines that impede learning and create stress. Their rules are either unclear or not enforced consistently, which causes the teacher to resort to confrontational methods like demanding, lecturing, and raising one's voice. Fun must be kept to a minimum in order to maintain control, and in response, students become bored, uninspired, and prone to cause trouble.

In classrooms where the balance of freedom and boundaries exists, students are motivated to actively participate in their learning. They're enjoying school too much to sacrifice a minute of their time by breaking rules and fulfilling consequences. If rules are broken, however, there is no negotiation, no debate, and no argument. They are simply enforced. Students are held accountable with a predetermined consequence that they don't like: being separated and held apart from the class that they love.

Like the hard/soft martial art of Goju-Ryu, the faithful use of freedom and boundaries is a nearly perfect combination in the hands of a teacher determined to create the best learning environment for his or her students.

Putting It Into Practice

1. Students respond best to a balance of freedom and boundaries, which is a characteristic shared by great teachers.

2. Clearly establish—through direct instruction, modeling, and role playing—unambiguous boundary lines of behavior.

3. Review your boundaries/rules/expectations daily.

4. Enforce your rules 100% of the time with the one consequence that all students dislike: separation from a class that they love.

5. Within your boundaries, allow students the freedom to be themselves and enjoy learning without worrying whether other students will interfere with this right.

Dream Class

Allow Freedom Within Boundaries

Show Them How

Build Rapport

Give Worthy Praise

Cultivate Independence

Transform Limiting Beliefs

Take Responsibility

Hold Students Accountable

Be A Great Storyteller

Help Shy Students Flourish

Treat The Cause, Not The Symptoms

Involve And Utilize Parents

Develop Maturity

Free Your Room, Free Your Mind

See The Best In Your Students

One Last Thing

We learn by example and by direct experience because there are real limits to the adequacy of verbal instruction.

—*Malcolm Gladwell*

Key #2

Show Them How

One morning, early in the school year, I had my students lined up shoulder-to-shoulder on one of the many yellow lines that criss-cross the playground. They were waiting for me as I walked onto the school grounds through the front gate. I was wearing a small backpack I borrowed from one of the students and was dressed in the school's uniform—a white polo shirt and blue slacks. My hair was combed in an exaggerated side part with thick gel, to add to the illusion of the role I was playing.

When I got within earshot of the class, I turned back toward the street and yelled, "Bye mom! See you after school! Love you!" The students giggled as I continued walking toward them. When I reached a small, gold-painted circle a few feet in front of their line, I stopped. This marked the spot where the students were to line up before school.

Detailed Modeling

Before the exercise began, I told my students that I wanted them to watch me carefully but to ignore me as I would be ignoring them. I stood on the spot and pretended to talk to other students in line until I pushed a button on my watch, triggering a beep that signified the morning bell. Immediately, I started walking the exact route I expected my students to take on their way to the classroom every morning.

> *Humor makes the activity more entertaining, and the students are more apt to pay close attention; they want to see what I'm going to do next.*

I continued to carry on in quiet conversation with my imaginary classmates as I walked. I also smiled and greeted those who passed by, in the manner I expected from my students. I talked with my imaginary friends about having my homework done in the proper way and about how I liked my teacher but thought he was a little crazy. This garnered a laugh from the students as they followed closely behind. I always add humor to these exercises. Humor makes the activity more entertaining, and the students are more apt to pay close attention; they want to see what I'm going to do next.

When I reached the bottom of the ramp leading into the classroom, I stopped and reminded my imaginary friends that we were not to talk from this point on until the teacher gave permission. I walked up the ramp, and as I approached the door, I reached just inside the room with my left hand and tapped a poster that read:

Learn Like A Champion Today

The poster is a play on a similar idea used by the University of Notre Dame football team. A rectangular wooden placard hangs outside the locker room at Notre Dame Stadium where the Fighting Irish play football. It is located at the bottom of the stairs leading out to the field, and each member of the team taps it on his way out. It's a tradition that goes back more than 20 years. It reads:

Play Like A Champion Today

I've only been using my version for ten or twelve years, but I've found it to be helpful in putting students in the proper frame of mind before entering the classroom. I refer to it often as a reminder of what each student's purpose is every time they walk in. They think it's cool and tap it enthusiastically.

Continuing my modeling exercise, I walked purposefully into the classroom, hung the backpack on its numbered hook, pulled out my homework notebook, checked the student mailboxes for any messages, and then sat down at my (a student's) desk.

Next, I pulled out my homework, checked that I had my name and correct date written neatly in the top right-hand corner, and placed it on the top left-hand corner of my desk.

Finally, I stood up, pushed in my chair, faced the American flag, and waited for the Pledge of Allegiance to begin—all of which I did with a look of mild concentration on my face. I wanted to communicate the idea of focusing on the present and the task at hand. Too many students arrive at school distracted and overly concerned about what others are doing.

Clarifying

After performing the pledge, the activity was over. I turned to the students who were crowded around me and said, "So, what do you think? It's simple enough, right? Does anyone have any questions?" After answering a few questions, I asked, "Is there anyone who doesn't know exactly what to do from the time you leave your ride in the morning until you're ready for the Pledge?"

I use this questioning technique often. By asking if there is anyone who *doesn't* know, the onus is on the students to speak up. This is another way of shifting the burden of responsibility over to students, which I've found brings out the best in them.

A Well-Oiled Machine

Now it was their turn. I took them just outside of the entrance to the school with their backpacks and had them go through the whole routine. I watched closely while occasionally giving reminders and suggestions. Every morning I'll watch them follow this routine before the start of the school day to make sure it is done correctly. I know this makes me sound like a taskmaster, but in reality, the students rarely stray from the script if it's modeled for them in detail. Furthermore, asking something of your students and then not checking to see that it's done properly is bad teaching.

The great thing about modeling in this manner is that you only have to do it one time. Rarely do I ever have to revisit a procedure again during the year. The few times I've had to reteach were because I didn't model thoroughly enough the first time.

I like my class to run like a well-oiled machine. If yours doesn't, I'll venture to guess that you haven't modeled the expectations you have for your class with as much detail. Surprisingly, I've never seen another teacher model in this way, and it boggles my mind as to why. It's incredibly powerful and effective.

If you want something done a certain way—and being an effective teacher, you'll want everything done a certain way—then you must explicitly show your students how. Otherwise, how are they going to know? Telling them how to do something isn't nearly as effective as showing them how to do it and then letting them practice. In fact, telling them isn't very effective at all.

A Memory Map

The precise modeling of how you want your students to behave, and of what you want them to do and when, will accelerate the learning of school and classroom procedures tenfold. Modeling exercises like the one described above create a memory map for your students. The humor and small details act as hooks to which they attach their memories. Often, I will fall down along the way or spill water down my shirt. It's funny at the time and holds their attention, but it also helps to embed in their memory the details of the procedure they're learning. With few exceptions, your students will emulate whatever you've modeled for them explicitly.

> **With few exceptions, your students will emulate whatever you've modeled for them explicitly.**

Include A Spirit Of Fun

I often find myself sitting in a student's chair, modeling one thing or another with the students gathered around. It works *so* much better than merely telling them and makes teaching easier and more enjoyable. I don't have to waste my time repeating myself and explaining the same things over and over again.

And students love this way of teaching. It's fun and participatory, makes learning and remembering procedures virtually effortless, and they always know exactly what is expected of them.

The key to its effectiveness is the use of specific detail combined with a dash of humor. I've never tried, but I don't believe modeling would work well without a spirit of fun. In the hands of an unenthusiastic teacher, the process would be excruciating for students and, as a result, ineffective.

Focus On Learning

I'll use this modeling technique with every classroom procedure, however minor. Imagine how much smoother and more effective your teaching will be if you don't have to waste time reminding, reteaching, or explaining procedural directions. Your students will know exactly what to do—and how to do it well—during every moment of the school day.

Children are craving to know what is expected of them, and detailed modeling clearly and definitively spells it out for them. Furthermore, the security in knowing what is expected will allow your students to focus on the primary goal of any classroom: learning.

Putting It Into Practice

1. Modeling is much more effective than voice instruction and infinitely more effective than no instruction at all.

2. Detailed modeling saves hours of time and eliminates confusion.

3. Detailed modeling of even the most mundane procedures best shows your students exactly how you want things (anything) done.

4. Humor and small details act as hooks along a memory map, further solidifying your students' understanding of your expectations.

5. Understanding your expectations of them will enable your students to focus on the primary goal of any successful classroom: learning.

Dream Class

Allow Freedom Within Boundaries

Show Them How

Build Rapport

Give Worthy Praise

Cultivate Independence

Transform Limiting Beliefs

Take Responsibility

Hold Students Accountable

Be A Great Storyteller

Help Shy Students Flourish

Treat The Cause, Not The Symptoms

Involve And Utilize Parents

Develop Maturity

Free Your Room, Free Your Mind

See The Best In Your Students

One Last Thing

*The key to successful leadership
is influence, not authority.*

—Ken Blanchard

Key #3

Build Rapport

Several years ago, I transferred to a new school to be closer to my home. A few weeks before the school year began, I received a call inviting me to lunch with two of my new colleagues. We met at a local Mexican restaurant.

After introducing ourselves, one of them reminded me that we had met before. A few months earlier, he had visited my classroom with a contingent of teachers and their principal to observe a lesson. I recalled that we had been playing a vocabulary review game.

I was playing the part of a game show host, and the students were having a blast. Circled into two groups, they were frantically rifling through individual letters of the alphabet written on index cards. I would read aloud a definition, and they had to come up with the correct word and spell it out by holding up the cards. The first team to spell the word correctly would earn the greater number of points.

There was a lot of laughing and cheering, and if the students were aware a group of adults were watching, they didn't let on.

I think it's valuable for students to have fun while learning, but with an important caveat. The fun must be shared by all, be within the rules, and never be at the expense of others. It must also match the appropriateness of the situation. On this day, the students were following, to a tee, the spirit of this message.

As the teachers began filing out of the room, their principal pulled me aside and said, "Why don't you come work for me next year? We have an opening in fourth grade." After checking my Thomas Guide and hearing many nice things about the surrounding community, I took her up on the offer.

Ruling With An Iron Fist

My new colleague told me at lunch that day that he enjoyed my lesson, but he wanted me to know that he wasn't the type of teacher to have fun with his class. He said he was more distant in his inter-actions with students. At the time, I wasn't sure why he was telling me this. If that was his style, it was okay with me. It was none of my business.

I came to know him as a knowledgeable teacher who was well pre-pared for his lessons. He was fair, consistent, and outwardly com-posed when addressing students. He seemed to be a caring teacher; he wanted the best for his students. But he was indeed distant and often stressed beneath his cool exterior.

As we got to know each other better, he confided in me that although he had good control of his class, he had to work hard at it—resorting to repeated calls to parents, stern lectures, frequent time-outs, and severe limitations of privileges.

His austere approach was wearing on his students. They were often bored and unhappy and, as a result, more likely to act up. Like many well-meaning teachers, he felt that he needed to rule his classroom with an iron fist to maintain control and get the most out of his students.

He must have noticed that my students were well behaved despite how happy they were, and how calm and relaxed I was, because he asked me for my advice. As delicately as I could, I suggested that if he loosened up some and started having more fun with his class, he would have better rapport with his students and wouldn't have to resort to using such stiff measures.

Rapport Makes Everything Easier

Undoubtedly, having good rapport with your students makes everything easier, especially with students who have a proclivity for behavior problems. Having a natural, trusting relationship with students is tremendously beneficial, but how is it best obtained?

> *Building rapport is an organic process that can backfire if the relationship is forced.*

Some teachers spend precious time outside of class with individual students trying to gain that trusting rapport—especially with those who struggle with behavior issues. They eat lunch with students, play recess games with them, or just sit and talk. Although time consuming, these activities can be helpful, but they're not always effective. Building rapport is an organic process that can backfire if the relationship is forced.

Despite these extra efforts, many teachers fall short of establishing a mutually satisfying relationship with every student and each year end up in a constant struggle with at least a few. Moreover, working outside of class to build better relationships can leave little time for anything else.

The Key To Building Rapport

Why does building rapport come naturally for some teachers and not for others? Why does classroom management come so easy to a select few, and others struggle? The answer resides in how your students feel about you. If the teaching persona you present to them is unlikable, then you will have a difficult time building rapport and will have little influence over the choices they make—other than by using some form of punishment.

> *If someone you don't like gives you advice, are you going to listen to it?*

Your students will make their choices because they want to or because of other outside influences, but they won't make them because of you. Your only options become being a strict disciplinarian and demanding respect and obedience or becoming a poor teacher and trying to get through the day.

Think about it. If someone you don't like gives you advice, are you going to listen to it? Or are you more likely to roll your eyes and ignore it? What if someone you admire gives you advice? Will you react differently? Presumably yes, and so will your students.

Weak Influence

How many times have you heard a teacher say, "I don't smile the first month (or two months, or trimester) of the school year?" Personally, I hear it every year. I also know teachers who almost never let their guard down, rarely smiling or showing any of their true personality throughout the school year.

The problem with this approach is that it will foil any attempt to build authentic rapport. If your students see you as an unsmiling, less-than-friendly person, building a trusting and influential relationship with them becomes nearly impossible. Furthermore, once you choose the role of the tough, stern teacher, you're stuck with it for the whole year—or even for a career—unless you learn a better way.

I'll give you a recent example. After having recess duty one morning, I was pushing an equipment rack loaded with hula-hoops, jump ropes, and kick balls off the playground and toward a storage room when two students from a neighboring classroom approached me. One of them asked, "Mr. Linsin, can we help you with the equipment this week?"

I said, "Sure, but you'll have to ask your teacher because you may be a few minutes late going back to class."

"Would you mind asking her for us?" they asked.

I thought the question was odd, so I replied, "No, I don't mind, but why don't you ask her?"

They looked at each other and said simultaneously, "She's scary."

Interestingly, this particular teacher works hard to make close connections with her students and even prides herself on it. She often pulls them aside for enthusiastic pep talks, hugs, and high fives. She buys them lunch occasionally and can be seen playing soccer with them outside. She also stays late after work and agonizes over her students' test scores. These are wonderful attributes. She truly cares about them and their future. But in the classroom she can be humorless.

She sets a demanding tone and occasionally will use a loud voice to intimidate. And despite her extra efforts at building rapport, she struggles with constant behavior issues. Several times she has said to me, "I don't know how much longer I can do this. I give and give and give, and they continue to disappoint me. They just don't care."

Given her persona in the classroom, when this teacher approaches students with an enthusiastic smile and offer of a high five, they're taken aback by it. They're confused by the contrast between the stern classroom teacher and this other person who desperately wants to bond with them. Personal interactions with the teacher then become awkward and even "scary." It's even more difficult for such a teacher to communicate with children who are shy or who have recurrent behavior problems.

How Best To Build Rapport

To make your job a lot easier and your teaching more effective, bring some fun and personality into your classroom on the very first day of school. Smile a lot. And when it comes to building rapport, fuggidaboudit! Let them come to you.

> *If you can create an enjoyable learning environment for your students, and your personality is consistently pleasant and good-humored, you have the keys to the kingdom.*

I'm not suggesting that you ignore your students, but you simply don't have to work hard trying to connect with them. Believe it or not, you're better off not giving too much time and effort to it. This may sound counterintuitive, but being overzealous can cause your students to feel uncomfortable and make you appear desperate. Desperation can ruin any relationship, and it will subvert any chance at lasting rapport with your students.

There is no reason to force a comfortable and trusting relationship. If you can create an enjoyable learning environment for your students, and your personality is consistently pleasant and good-humored, you have the keys to the kingdom. *They* will want to get to know *you* better, making influential relationships with students unforced, natural, and easy.

Now when you approach students to give compliments or high fives, it will mean something to them. If you need to talk with one or more of your students about poor choices they've made, and they like you and love being in your class, you have real leverage. You'll have their attention when you look them in the eye and say, "I'm disappointed in you." Your words will have an effect.

An easy rapport with students is simply a byproduct of a well-liked teacher and a happy classroom. So put a smile on your face and take advantage of this powerful fulcrum. Combined with a firm discipline plan, you can be among those teachers for whom building rapport with students, as well as classroom management, looks so easy.

Putting It Into Practice

1. Having rapport with students gives you powerful leverage and influence and makes everything easier—especially behavior management.

2. It's difficult to build rapport with students if your teaching persona is unlikable.

3. Add fun and a smile to your classroom the first day of school.

4. There is no need to consciously try to build rapport. If your personality is pleasant and good-humored and you create an enjoyable learning experience for your students, good rapport will happen naturally.

Dream Class

*When a child does something
well, commendation
is a powerful tool.*

—John Wooden

Key #4

Give Worthy Praise

For the past few years, I have organized an in-school hockey league for fifth graders. Typically, we have between eight and ten teams competing in two divisions. We have a regular season consisting of about 25 games for each team, divisional playoffs, and a championship. In October we hold the first meeting for those interested in being on a team, and the season runs until March, when the playoffs begin. During that first meeting, without fail, I get the same question: "What do we get if we play?"

To be honest, I have a hard time answering it. The short answer is that they get nothing—at least nothing material. However, the benefits of playing on a sports team are endless. They include camaraderie, sportsmanship, competition, perseverance, and much more. These internal rewards are best experienced; explaining them doesn't do them justice.

In many youth sports leagues across the country, every player gets a trophy whether his or her team wins a championship or not. I assume that organizers do this to avoid harming the players' self-esteem. If no one team is singled out for excellence and awarded because of their superior performance, then nobody gets their feelings hurt. Awarding every player puts everyone on the same plane. Everyone is a winner. If you show up, you get a trophy. But isn't showing up an expectation for anyone who is on a team?

> *In the end, it's the act of pursuing the goal that holds the greatest reward.*

One of the wonderful benefits of playing sports is that they are a microcosm of life. We learn how to win with dignity, overcome disappointment and loss, and rely on our friends and teammates for support. Collectively striving toward the objective of winning a championship enhances these life lessons. This should be the focus. The intrinsic rewards that come from winning and losing as a team while in pursuit of a worthy goal are reward enough.

When only the championship winning team gets the prize, it underscores the worthiness of the pursuit. In the end, it's the act of pursuing the goal that holds the greatest reward. It is here where life lessons are learned. To cheapen them by awarding everyone a plastic trophy shows a misunderstanding of where true value lies.

Although not harmful in the short term, handing out trophies to all participants sends a subtle message: fulfilling the most basic expectation—merely showing up—is worthy of special recognition. Is this the message we want to send to our children? I don't believe so. If we lower the bar to recognize minimal achievement, then that's all we'll get. Moreover, presenting everyone with an obligatory award devalues genuine accomplishment and dampens the spirit of its pursuit.

The Improper Use Of Praise In The Classroom

Just as rewarding trophies indiscriminately waters down the value of youth sports, so too does the misuse of praise in the classroom. I hear teachers praising children daily for doing what is, in our society, a common expectation. For example, if you praise a student for pushing in his or her chair, you are creating in that student an expectation of recognition for something that, frankly, isn't worthy of it. This reinforces an expectation of praise based on nothing. Your students will become so accustomed to a pat on the back for accomplishing the mundane that it loses its meaning.

Have you ever said to a student who was sitting quietly, "Great job, Thomas! I love how you're sitting at your desk." I hope not, although I hear it all the time. Whenever you use praise like this, you lower the expectations for that which is truly praiseworthy. If Thomas accomplishes something special—let's say he writes an outstanding essay, one that is considerably better than anything he has written before—then you'll have to organize a parade to create relative distance between the praise given for sitting quietly and the praise for his essay.

What will Thomas think when you say, "Great essay, Thomas!" He will likely assume that in his teacher's value system, both efforts were equal. This begs the question: if that is so, why should Thomas try to excel? It would have to be because of some internal motivation or other outside influence, but it would unlikely be because of you. Empty praise will limit your influence.

Use Politeness Instead

When I was enrolled in a teacher education program, working toward my credential, I was told to catch students doing something good (i.e., doing what they were supposed to be doing) and then praise them for it. This will not only make the student feel good, I was told, but other students will notice and do the same. My thinking at the time is the same as it is now: why would I do that? To what end? Praise used like this lowers the bar, has no real meaning, and is dishonest. Is it really a "great job" to sit quietly? Is it even possible to do a great job while sitting quietly?

If you're using praise in this manner to influence others, like to sit quietly, there is a better way. Good old-fashioned politeness will get the same result without dumbing down the effectiveness of praise. For example, "Thanks for sitting quietly, Thomas." You are modeling the appropriate use of good manners, and sitting quietly is worthy of a thank you. It's honest and doesn't involve saying something that you don't believe to be true.

> *By saying thank you, you're not telling Thomas that sitting quietly is in any way an accomplishment. You're simply thanking him for doing what is expected.*

By saying thank you, you're not telling Thomas that sitting quietly is in any way an accomplishment. You're simply thanking him for doing what is expected. *Now* when you praise him for his essay, your recognition will mean something and will encourage him to further pursue excellence in your classroom.

Exceptions

I realize there are exceptions. Notable, are students with attention disorders and some types of learning disabilities. And occasionally you may encounter students without identified disabilities who, at times, need to be praised for something as simple as sitting quietly. For a majority of children, however, this is an expectation.

Another exception is when you are introducing something new into your program. At the start of the school year, when I'm modeling classroom procedures, I may praise students for completing a procedure correctly for the first time. After the initial learning, however, it's an expectation.

Praise Helps Communicate What You Want

Used properly, praise can be a powerful motivator. Children love to be recognized for doing something well, and it's important that you do so. Never let an accomplishment or a good deed pass without your acknowledgement. Ignoring exceptional behavior or performance is as detrimental as empty praise. Praise will help you steer your students in the direction of excellence. If you withhold it from them, you will have a harder time communicating what you want.

> *Ignoring exceptional behavior or performance is as detrimental as empty praise.*

I worked for a principal who, during his first couple of months on the job, was attempting to establish school safety rules and guidelines, as well as new lunch times and procedures. The school had become lax in these areas, and he wanted to tighten things up.

Several years before, I had created a list of playground safety rules and duty guidelines for teachers based on my observations. Upon hearing his plans, I dug up this document, updated it, and presented it to him.

A couple of weeks later, he unveiled his plans to the staff, which included my exact document. I had no problem with this in the least; I wanted to help. But he never acknowledged me for sharing it. Naturally, I concluded that he must not have valued the help, and from then on I was more reluctant to go beyond my duties in the classroom—not because I was unwilling, but because I didn't know if he wanted or appreciated the help. It's the same with your students. If you don't recognize their good work, then how will they know what you want from them?

A Time To Praise

Much has been debated regarding how best to encourage healthy self-esteem in children. In my experience, the only way people feel good about themselves is when they accomplish something that is challenging for them, do something they didn't know they could do, or help someone.

You must be vigilant in watching for these actions and achievements in your students, and when you see them, be heartfelt in your praise. Shine a light on their good work. Through the appropriate use of praise, you can strongly influence your students' motivation to learn, their determination to succeed, and their sense of altruism toward other students.

Note:

Praise doesn't have to be effusive or over the top to be effective. Often, a measured but sincere act of commendation will have greater impact. A nod of the head, a fist bump, eye contact with a smile; when your intentions are pure, the smallest gesture can produce a powerful effect.

Putting It Into Practice

1. The proper use of praise will direct your students toward the behavior you want.

2. Break the habit of praising students for doing what is a common expectation.

3. Thank students with a smile for doing what is expected.

4. What may be a common expectation for most students, may not be for everyone.

5. Those with attention disorders or special needs may need different criteria for what constitutes a common expectation.

6. Never fail to recognize and praise students for good performance.

Dream Class

Don't wish for someone else to do later what you can do now.

— *Wynton Marsalis*

Key #5

Cultivate Independence

One morning the principal strolled into my classroom unannounced. Like many good principals, she preferred to get out of her office and into the classrooms as often as she could. As she walked in, the students were beginning their independent math work. I had finished my lesson a few minutes before and was walking around the room looking over shoulders.

I like to spend a moment or two watching each student to ensure that they're doing the work as it was explained during the lesson. The last thing I want is for them to go home, sit down to do their homework, and not fully understand how. As I watch the students work, I typically don't say anything other than a periodic, "Looks good."

On this day, like most days, the students were quiet and focused. Having finished my rounds, I looked up to find the principal standing next to me. I had a good relationship with her and was comfortable doing my job as I saw fit. She said hello and then made a comment about how independent the students were. Then she asked, "Do they ever ask for help?"

"Occasionally," I answered, "if my lesson wasn't clear enough."

She smiled and mouthed goodbye as she left the room.

Only Half The Story

The explanation I gave her was honest, but only half the story. Some of my methods are unconventional and can take time to explain—time a busy principal doesn't usually have, although I'm always happy to oblige. It's true that I'm exceedingly careful to make my lessons clear. When teaching math, for example, I actively look for and cut out anything superfluous and leave only the essentials needed to correctly solve each problem. I've discovered that this streamlined method of teaching leads to better conceptual understanding and, as a result, better performance.

> *I've discovered that this streamlined method of teaching leads to better conceptual understanding and, as a result, better performance.*

I like to proceed in a step-by-step manner, listing steps on an easel for students to refer to. I explain each step simply and thoroughly while giving detailed examples. If satisfied with the responses to my accompanying questions, I'll ask the students to solve a few problems on their own. To do this, I'll write a problem on a 10" x 12" whiteboard and hold it up for everyone to see. The students, in turn, make their computations on their own whiteboards. When they're finished and ready to reveal their answers, we count to three and they hold them up. For the next minute or so, I'll bounce around the room while quickly scanning and checking their answers.

The students love doing this because it's a lot of fun. I'll point at their correct answers and yell out, "You got it!" "Bang!" or "Pow!" Many students will write silly messages or draw smiley faces for me under their answers. If I find a wrong answer, I'll give extra coaching to that one student on the spot or while they are solving the next problem.

We continue in this way until I'm satisfied that every student is ready to work independently. The idea is to send them off to do independent work only when they fully grasp the concepts presented during the lesson. To do otherwise is setting them up for failure. This is a standard teaching method, but again, it's only half the story. The other half is this: after they begin independent work, I rarely help individual students.

Slow To Help

When my students are doing independent work, I'll walk around and check their progress, but I'm reluctant to help and will do so only under certain circumstances. I know this sounds blasphemous to many teachers, but I strongly believe that, in most cases, when you kneel down beside a student to help, you are doing more harm than good. By doing so, you are encouraging your students to:

 Tune you out during lessons.

 Relinquish responsibility for their learning.

 Become dependent on you.

Nearly all teachers are quick to help and many would blanch at refusing to do so, but it's in your best interest and that of your students if you refrain. This may be a harsh message for some to accept because it gives the impression of indifference, or even callousness, but this assumption is far from true. In fact, minimizing individual help is a great thing to do for your students.

> *If you are a chronic helper with your students, I'll bet my house that you have a lot of daydreamers.*

Why would your students feel the urgency to listen to, participate in, and closely follow your lessons if they know that you're willing to teach them the same material individually? They wouldn't and they don't. If you are a chronic helper with your students, I'll bet my house that you have a lot of daydreamers. If you want attentiveness and interest, make your lessons simple (not easy), combine them with a touch of fun, and when it comes time for independent work, be slow to help.

I'm clear with my students that after the lesson ends, for the most part, they're on their own. I'm also honest as to why I'm reluctant to help. The students, in response, become much more participatory in the lessons and ask deeper, more probing questions. It's not uncommon for them to ask for one last example despite having already proven to me their understanding of the material. Only after answering every question and getting agreement that they're ready, will we begin individual practice.

This method of teaching works because the teacher is shifting the burden of responsibility for learning to the students, where it belongs. Too many teachers, in their zeal to be the kind of teacher who will do anything for their students, end up doing too much for them—to the detriment of the students.

Other Benefits

Encouraging independence in your students also makes your job easier. It removes the stress of jumping from one student to another, reteaching something that you taught for the whole class minutes earlier. It also dramatically reduces homework problems, improves performance, and boosts academic self-confidence.

As a side benefit, by helping individual students less, you'll be compelled to make your lessons easy to understand and as engrossing as possible.

Mental Muscles

There is no getting around the importance of stamina and hard work in the success of your students, and they must be given ample time to strengthen these mental muscles. Set them up for success with clear, straightforward, and focused lessons, and then get out of their way. Allow them plenty of time to practice and wrestle with the presented material without interference.

Special Circumstances

There *are* times when I sit down and work with individual students, particularly during periods of reading and writing, and those with certain learning disabilities. But there is a difference between jump-starting a student's thinking with pointed questions and reteaching something that has already been taught.

A Checking System

Early in my career, I noticed that many of the mistakes made on math tests were caused by carelessness, which is a sign of dependency on others. Students were making mistakes that had nothing to do with their math ability. Many were losing a full letter grade because of it. So after reading a book about helicopter pilots in Vietnam whose lives depended on their hyper-attentiveness, I devised a system.

I created a large poster with the words "check," "recheck," and "check it again" written in bold letters. I hung the poster up and started hammering this mantra home. I stressed that after finishing a test, each student needed to go through all three steps before turning it in. As a reminder, at the bottom of every test I added three boxes:

☑ *CHECK*

☑ *RECHECK*

☑ *CHECK IT AGAIN*

Each time the students checked their work, they would put a check mark in the corresponding box. After checking the last box, they would approach the front of the room where I placed a plastic in-box on a kidney-shaped table. On the floor, five feet in front of the table, I affixed a length of masking tape about three feet long. The students would stop at the tape and make a final decision. If they were 100% happy with their test, they would step across the line and turn it in. If not, they could return to their desks and work on whatever was nagging them.

Students quickly buy into this checking system because they see immediate proof of its effectiveness in the form of higher grades and better test scores. It also instills in them an important life skill they can take with them into the future.

Every successful organization, from business to sports, has in common a relentless pursuit of excellence. As classroom teachers, why should we be any different?

After starting this process of helping individuals less and adding the checking system, my students began looking inward when confronted with learning challenges rather than relying on me. Eventually, they became relentless problem solvers, taking great pride in their ability to work through academic conundrums on their own and with their classmates.

A Two-Way Street

The confidence students acquire because of their new level of independence can be empowering. They think, I did this myself! And they really did. There was no teacher kneeling next to them with a baby spoon.

> *Focus your efforts on creating and delivering first-class lessons, and stop shouldering the burden of what are your students' responsibilities.*

I tell my students often, "It's my job to teach, and I'll make sure you have the best, most fun, and most exciting lessons in the world. However, it's your job and responsibility to listen and learn what is being taught and then to practice with great effort. It's a two-way street. I'm giving my best for you, and you have to do the same for me."

Let Your Students Do Their Job

The more you can pass the responsibility for learning over to your students the better. Focus your efforts on creating and delivering first-class lessons, and stop shouldering the burden of what are your students' responsibilities. Your goal should be to increasingly place more and more of the onus on your students. Not only will this allow you to breathe easier, but more importantly, it will raise the levels of learning, retention, and performance in your students.

A great way to start is to cut back on individual help and add a checking system. Tighten up your lessons by eliminating the fat and focusing laser-like on your objectives. Finally, make your lessons participatory, include an element of fun, and then allow your students to do *their* job.

Dependent Students Make Teaching Stressful

Dependence is a habit students pick up from the adults in their life, including teachers. Ironically, it's one of the things teachers complain about the most—and for good reason. Dependent students make teaching stressful and less enjoyable.

Doing too much for your students will drive you crazy and hurt their chances for success. Cultivate independence in your students, and you will be giving them, as well as yourself, an invaluable gift.

Putting It Into Practice

1. Encouraging independence makes your job easier and improves learning, retention, and performance.

2. Create lessons that are simply taught, engaging, and participatory.

3. Only send students off to do independent work when they fully grasp the material presented in your lesson.

4. When you kneel down to help individual students during independent work time, you are doing more harm than good.

5. Provide your students with a checking system to cut down on careless mistakes.

Dream Class

Allow Freedom Within Boundaries

Show Them How

Build Rapport

Give Worthy Praise

Cultivate Independence

Transform Limiting Beliefs

Take Responsibility

Hold Students Accountable

Be A Great Storyteller

Help Shy Students Flourish

Treat The Cause, Not The Symptoms

Involve And Utilize Parents

Develop Maturity

Free Your Room, Free Your Mind

See The Best In Your Students

One Last Thing

Leadership is communicating to people their worth and potential so clearly that they come to see it in themselves.

—Steven Covey

Key #6

Transform Limiting Beliefs

A girl named Veronica became one of my most memorable students. She was in my third-grade class during only my second year of teaching, and she single-handedly changed how I viewed my role as a teacher. She sat in the front of the classroom with a winsome smile on her face. One morning during the first week of school, she called me over to her desk and told me decidedly that she wasn't smart and that she didn't "get math." I thanked her for letting me know and asked her to come by the classroom before school the next day so that we could take a look at her math book together.

She arrived the next morning with her smile and her math book, and we proceeded to tackle the homework assigned from the day before. It quickly became apparent to me that she was bright. She listened well and asked smart questions. But she was unsuccessful in her attempts to solve the problems without my close guidance. Tellingly, and despite her outwardly sunny disposition, she peppered our conversation with negative self-talk. The image she held of herself as a student was inaccurately low. I concluded that she didn't need any extra help or tutoring. What she needed was convincing that she was indeed smart and that excelling in school was within her capabilities.

A quick glance at her previous records showed undeniably that she wasn't a very good student, but I was certain that she had the ability to excel. So I spent the next several months endeavoring to change how she saw herself. After a few short weeks, it began working. Her grades improved, and her smile turned into one of confidence.

A few minutes later, as the news began sinking in, tears rolled down her face, and I caught a glimpse of the smile Veronica had inherited.

Near the end of the school year, I received a letter from the school district informing me that Veronica was to be tested for the district's Gifted And Talented Education (GATE) program. Her high grades combined with excellent standardized test scores made her eligible for testing.

A couple of weeks later, I received the news that she had qualified, and I scheduled a conference with her mother. After her mom sat down, I informed her that her daughter had been identified as a GATE student and was going to need a specific plan designed to challenge her. At first she didn't believe me and asked, "Are you serious?" Then she added, "Do you think they made a mistake?"

A few minutes later, as the news began sinking in, tears rolled down her face, and I caught a glimpse of the smile Veronica had inherited. It was a great moment. I remained Veronica's teacher for two more years as I moved up in grade levels and was fortunate enough to witness her continue to grow into an outstanding student and confident person.

A Broader Experiment

After that first year with Veronica, I began thinking. If I applied the same techniques I used with Veronica to the entire class, what could they be capable of? How exciting would it be to affect all of my students so profoundly? And could these feelings of confidence and inner belief rub off on one another?

> *They were always capable of reaching greater academic heights. All I did was convince them that they could.*

The following year my students' grades improved markedly, and their standardized test scores sky-rocketed. Teachers began showing up at my door, at the insistence of the principal, wanting to know how I was doing it. The truth was, I didn't really know what to tell them. It wasn't so much that I didn't know how or why my students were doing so well, it was more that I didn't think they would believe me. The fact is, it was only my third year of teaching. My lessons weren't particularly dynamic, the thematic units I used were copied from more experienced teachers, and I spent a considerable amount of time laughing and joking with my students.[†]

So how did they do it? How were my students able to raise their test scores and elevate their grades beyond anything they had done in the past? Like Veronica, the answer could be found within the students themselves. They were always capable of reaching greater academic heights. All I did was convince them that they could. I simply helped them change the perceptions they held of themselves as students.

How Do Your Students See Themselves?

All children have an image of themselves as the kind of student they

---

[†]   Using humor in the classroom is addressed in **One Last Thing** found on page 179.

are, based on what they believe to be true. In many, if not most, circumstances, that image is below their actual ability level. They acquire these limiting beliefs about themselves from a variety of sources, including parents, teachers, siblings, peers, their neighborhood, and news and entertainment media.

If you can draw your students away from this erroneous view and enable them to see themselves as they really are (i.e., their true capabilities), you will notice a major shift in their attitude toward learning and a tangible change in their performance.

A Change In Thinking

The idea is to convince your students to believe that they are capable of performing much better—not sometime in the future, but right now. The first and most critical step is for you to believe in your heart that your students are capable of more than they're showing—that they are not the students they think they are. The words you use and the decisions you make will flow from this belief.

This is a much more dramatic difference in thinking than merely believing your students can improve. It is knowing that they are better students *right now* than they are demonstrating—not because they're not giving enough effort, but because the image they have of themselves doesn't match their capabilities. This isn't about imploring them to work harder, or instilling false confidence, or merely trying to "raise expectations." It is a wholesale change in the image they have of themselves as students, which is congruent with their performance. In other words, they will always perform consistent with how they see themselves. Change the image, and their performance will change with it.

In the 1920's, psychologist and schoolteacher Prescott Lecky, who later consulted a teenaged John F. Kennedy, conducted extensive research into this area of academic success and self-image. After thousands of experiments with children, he concluded that poor grades in school are nearly always related to a student's self-concept.

How To Improve Your Students' Academic Self-image

The following is a list of techniques that are effective in changing your students' academic self-image into one that more closely matches their true abilities:

♦See the many everyday tasks of learning as goals to be reached. Define them as goals for your students, and then track their pursuit and eventual attainment of them. Reaching goals—and making a point of acknowledging their achievement—will help your students realize what they're capable of.

♦Help your students understand that if they can do one thing well, there is no reason why they can't succeed in other areas as well. The attitudes they bring with them to tasks that they're good at should also be present when tackling challenges that they perceive to be more difficult for them.

♦Always behave as though it's a foregone conclusion that your students will excel.

♦Tell your students directly every day that you believe they're smart and capable of performing at a higher level. Spoken with sincerity and fervor, and coming from an authoritative source like a trusted teacher, this can be a powerful message.

♦Appear incredulous when you witness work or performance that you know is below their capabilities, and don't accept it. Tell them, "This isn't you. Go back and do it again like you and I both know you can."

♦Teach your students that their past doesn't have to determine their future. Tell them that you don't care what they have done in the past. It doesn't mean a thing. Today is a new day and another chance to be successful.

◆Never accept failure in your students or let them accept it in themselves. Failure is nothing more than being unprepared. It's important that you prove to them that when they're prepared they succeed.

◆Search high and low for success, however small, and then show your students the proof. When they succeed and perform at the level you expect, point it out emphatically. Prove to them their high level of ability using their own work. Show them their work and say, "This is it. This is what I'm talking about. This is what you're capable of. You're an excellent student. Now go show me more great work!"

> *Search high and low for success, however small, and then show your students the proof.*

◆Forbid and strictly guard against negative thinking, complaining, whining, and defeatist attitudes from your students. They are destroyers of academic self-image. With them comes sure failure.

◆Be cognizant of your own negative thoughts, attitudes, and feelings, and don't bring them with you to school. No matter how hard you try, you won't be able to hide them, and they will manifest themselves in subtle ways that will quell your students' progress.

◆Before a test or a significant assignment, take a few minutes and have your students picture themselves succeeding. Talk them through a visualization—or movie in their mind—of them performing the steps to completion and then receiving the grade they want. They have to see it in their mind's eye first before it becomes a reality.

◆Show your students specifically what a successful student looks like—their habits, preparation, organization, listening and speaking skills, and time management. Keep their thoughts on this image through lessons, role-playing, detailed modeling, and frequent reminders.

•Never use empty praise or flattery in a false attempt to boost self-esteem. This is antithetical to the authentic transformative power of discovering what one is truly capable of.

> *Last and most important, deliver your message with passion.*

•Last and most important, deliver your message with passion. The amount of passion you can muster demonstrates to your students the level of belief you have in them.

Our Beliefs Help Determine Our Future

When I was twelve or thirteen years old, I played on an ice hockey team. The organization I played for had trouble finding a coach for our team, so in the beginning a few parent volunteers supervised practice. Eventually, they found a coach who came to meet us after our first game. We lost by a lot. The score was 12-0, or thereabouts, and we were clearly overmatched in the league we were playing in.

I was sitting on a bench in the locker room with my teammates when Rob, the new coach, walked in. After introducing himself, the first thing he said was, "Hey guys, don't worry about tonight. It was the first game, no big deal. I can guarantee you this. We will make the playoffs." I remember glancing around at my teammates as we exchanged puzzled looks. Who is this guy, I thought? Didn't he see the game? We were terrible. How could we possibly make the playoffs?

After losing our first half dozen games, we reeled off ten wins in a row and found ourselves in the locker room dressing for our first playoff game. Was there a mysterious force at work that supernaturally made us into better players? Not in the least. We were the same players we were before, except our coach helped us replace a losing image with one that was consistent with our true ability. This change didn't in any way guarantee that we would win every game. It simply allowed us to play to our maximum ability. It's the same with your students. Essentially, you're helping them get out of their own way, freeing them to perform at the highest level they're capable of.

We lost our playoff game, but I looked at my hockey coach in a different light. In fact, I looked at everything differently. The lesson was this: our beliefs about ourselves can greatly affect future results. This isn't some new age mumbo-jumbo. It's nothing more than realizing that negative perceptions of ourselves can sabotage success.

I know firsthand that if we can help our students see a true picture of themselves and their abilities, then we will witness a giant leap in academic performance and set them firmly on the path that leads to success and opportunity.

Putting It Into Practice

1. All children have an image of themselves as the kind of student they are, based on what they believe to be true. Often, this belief is inaccurately low.

2. Believe in your heart that your students are capable of performing at a higher level *right now*.

3. Follow the list of techniques that help transform the current image your students have of themselves into one that matches their true capabilities.

4. Realize that your students will perform only to the level they see themselves and no higher. Thus, it's critical that you concentrate on raising this image to the level of their true ability, which for most students will result in a considerable jump in performance.

Dream Class

Allow Freedom Within Boundaries

Show Them How

Build Rapport

Give Worthy Praise

Cultivate Independence

Transform Limiting Beliefs

Take Responsibility

Hold Students Accountable

Be A Great Storyteller

Help Shy Students Flourish

Treat The Cause, Not The Symptoms

Involve And Utilize Parents

Develop Maturity

Free Your Room, Free Your Mind

See The Best In Your Students

One Last Thing

You've gotta stop wearing your wishbone where your backbone oughta be.

—Elizabeth Gilbert

Key #7

Take Responsibility

I t was 8:05 in the morning, ten minutes after the morning bell, and I was standing several feet outside of a kindergarten classroom. It was typical for me to wait until the teacher opened the door, signaling that she was ready for me to take her students. After waiting another five minutes, however, I opened the door myself, concerned she had forgotten that it was time for her students to come with me for their weekly physical education lesson.[†]

As I walked in, I noticed a few students sitting on the rug in front of her chair, ready to begin the day. Others were in various stages of putting their things away, and the rest she was trying to herd toward the rug. Frazzled, she looked up at me and said, "Sorry, they're crazy today. It has taken them ten minutes just to sit down so I can take roll."

"No problem, I'll take them whenever you're ready."

[†]   In addition to being a classroom teacher, I've also worked as a PE teacher.

After getting her students to sit on their numbers, which were embossed on individual carpet squares, she took roll and then looked back up at me. "They're all yours," she said. "Again, I don't know what the deal is with them. I know they're not great most of the time, but today..."

> *"The students don't decide how they're going to behave, we do."*

I lined the students up and got them quiet as the teacher began doing paperwork at her desk. I really liked this teacher. She was a friendly person with a quick smile, and I felt comfortable around her. I led the students out of the room and instructed the leader of the line to stop at a predetermined spot on the sidewalk about 30 feet from the room. I reached back with one hand to close the door while still watching the class. As I did, I instinctively leaned into the classroom to say something to the teacher.

Teachers Decide

Ordinarily, I don't say anything to other teachers about how they run their classrooms, and I think this is a good policy. Although I'm always happy to help, unless asked, it's none of my business. In the past, however, this teacher has shared with me how much she disliked her job and longed to either quit or transfer to a school located in an affluent suburb. So I leaned in and said, "The students don't decide how they're going to behave, we do."

She sighed and said, "I know you're probably right. It's just easier to blame them."

I don't think this teacher fully understood what I meant or was aware of this fact: there are teachers who have happy, well-behaved, and polite students year after year. It doesn't matter who is in their classroom. They decide how their students behave, not the students. This point is lost on too many teachers who believe the opposite: that the students dictate what kind of class they have and how each day goes. Countless times I've heard variations of the following:

> *I have a tough class this year. The administration dumped on me. I'll just have to get through it.*

> *My students call out all the time. It drives me crazy, but I have a needy group this year.*

> *They're so talkative today. I don't know what has gotten into them. It must be Friday.*

> *I was told that the incoming class of fourth graders are wild. It's going to be a long year.*

> *My class is so rowdy this week. They're out of their seats all the time. I guess it's the rainy weather.*

> *This year's class doesn't listen as well as the class I had last year. I hope next year is better. I'm crossing my fingers.*

Whenever I hear statements like these, I always think the same thing: the teacher has accepted a level of behavior management that is far below what is possible and most effective for optimal learning. The fact is, you have the power to influence your class—whoever they are and whatever the circumstances—and mold them into the well-behaved students you desire.

It's The Teacher

It starts with taking responsibility for everything that happens in your classroom, including your students' behavior. If they're not behaving the way you want them to, it's because of how you're managing your class. It's not about the students. It's about you!

If you believe you're at the mercy of your students, then you're severely limiting your potential effectiveness. This type of thinking will undermine everything you do as a teacher and leave you powerless to improve.

> *As an excuse you may hear, "Well, the personalities just didn't mix." Baloney. The previous teacher was ineffective.*

Exceptional teachers hear a variation of one particular comment from other teachers year after year. It's an irksome remark, about which the teacher can do little without risking professional decorum. Without fail it comes at least once and often several times a year. It goes like this: "You're so lucky. You have such a good class. I wish I could trade students with you."

The standard response is something like, "Yes, they are a nice class. Thanks." This is a good way to respond because it ends the conversation quickly. The exceptional teacher, however, would love to respond truthfully by saying, "Have you ever noticed that I have a good class every year? Maybe it's not the students. Maybe the students are the way they are because of me." Of course, they don't respond this way. It would appear spiteful and sound egotistical, but it's absolutely true. It's not the students. It's the teacher.

A student's behavior can change, sometimes drastically, from one year to the next because of the teacher. This isn't news. It happens on every campus. A student with behavior issues one school year can become well behaved, or considerably better, the next. As an excuse you may hear, "Well, the personalities just didn't mix." Baloney. The previous teacher was ineffective. Personality had nothing to do with it.

When you put away the excuses and take responsibility for your classroom, good things begin to happen. Taking responsibility is the impetus for making the changes needed to gain strong influence with your students and surefire control of your class. The moment you stop justifying for your students' unwanted behavior, you're left with the cold, hard truth: "It really isn't the students, it's me. And I need to learn some new skills." This realization, however, will remove the ceiling on your potential to impact students and render it limitless.

Strengthen Your Authority

Regardless of who you are, there will always be challenges—especially in the beginning of the year when you're setting up your program.

> *Every time you send a student away, you weaken your authority. Taking care of it yourself, by holding the student accountable, strengthens it.*

However, when a student decides to make a bad choice and stray outside of your boundaries, you don't throw your hands up and say, "Well, Yvette is with her dad (or mom) this week."[†] Excuses like this amount to giving up on her (as well as yourself), so too does sending her to the office.

The only reason you should ever send a student to the office is if you need to document dangerous behavior. Otherwise, you handle it yourself. When you send a student to the principal, you are announcing to that student, to the rest of your class, and to the principal that you don't have full command of your classroom. Furthermore, it undermines your ability to handle future problems. Every time you send a student away, you weaken your authority. Taking care of it yourself, by holding the student accountable, strengthens it.

---

†   I have heard this comment many times, and I know it can be difficult for kids to live in two households following a divorce. It's important that we are sensitive to what is happening in our students' lives outside of school. It does not, however, excuse poor behavior.

Create The Class You Really Want

It is solely your responsibility to create an atmosphere in your classroom where all students can learn without interference. It's their right. If there are students in your room who are disrupting that process by chatting with their friends, don't chalk it up to them being a talkative group. Instead, stop them immediately and reteach your expectations. Be clear about what you want and accept nothing less. They're a talkative group because their teacher allows them to be.

When you choose to take responsibility for your classroom—the successes as well as the failures, the good and the not so good—you become a better teacher instantly. Accepting that you alone conduct the orchestra will free you from the bonds that hold so many teachers back:

Making or accepting excuses for misbehavior.

Teachers who choose to ignore the 101 excuses and outside circumstances that are used to explain away disruptive behavior, and instead focus on solutions and possibilities, have the power to create the class they really want.

Regardless of who is on your roster, you can have, and should expect, polite and well-behaved students. It's doable, and you're wrong to think otherwise. There are teachers quietly doing it every day. You'll know because they are the "lucky" ones who have a good class every year.

Putting It Into Practice

1. You can have happy, well-behaved, and polite students in your classroom year after year.

2. You are not at the mercy of your students. You can influence and mold them into the class you desire.

3. Only send students to the office for dangerous behavior. Otherwise, you handle behavior problems yourself by holding students accountable.

4. Take responsibility for everything that happens in your classroom and for your students' behavior. Doing so will give you the power to create the class you really want.

Dream Class

Allow Freedom Within Boundaries

Show Them How

Build Rapport

Give Worthy Praise

Cultivate Independence

Transform Limiting Beliefs

Take Responsibility

Hold Students Accountable

Be A Great Storyteller

Help Shy Students Flourish

Treat The Cause, Not The Symptoms

Involve And Utilize Parents

Develop Maturity

Free Your Room, Free Your Mind

See The Best In Your Students

One Last Thing

The quality of strength lined with tenderness is an unbeatable combination.

—Maya Angelou

Key #8

Hold Students Accountable

The importance of accountability is bandied about liberally in our schools, but it's rarely used properly. Most teachers will tell you that holding students accountable is a priority, but too often it's used merely as a threat or as a last resort. There is some fear associated with using accountability as a behavior management method. Some teachers are afraid they will appear intolerant or inflexible if they don't allow a certain amount of wiggle room. Others have every intention of holding students accountable for undesirable behavior, but in the end don't keep their word. I believe that having vague or movable boundary lines of accountability is detrimental and unfair to children and causes an undue air of tension in the classroom.

Who Is In Charge?

I taught next door to a teacher who had classroom rules posted, but she referred to them only intermittently. Instead, her fourth-grade classroom was governed by open debate. Because she didn't have clear boundaries of accountability, she resorted to empty threats, criticism, and arguing to motivate her students to behave as she desired. The result was a tense classroom and an exhausted teacher.

A student named Allen rebelled against this form of classroom management. He challenged her on nearly every point and was determined to wrest control of the class from her. He was often successful, and taking up his cue, some of the other students began behaving in a similar way.

As part of a music and art rotation, Allen was scheduled to become part of my classroom on Friday afternoons. After watching his antics from a distance, I was looking forward to the challenge of having him under my supervision. His teacher approached me prior to the first day of rotations and told me that Allen did his best when given lots of leeway. She also mentioned that I should send him to the office if I needed to. I didn't say so, but I knew that neither option was going to work for me. Allen was going to have to follow my rules just like everyone else.

Let Your Consequences Do Their Job

Within five minutes of hearing me explain the classroom rules, Allen was up and wandering about the room. I had art supplies organized and set up for the lesson, and he was picking them up and tossing them in his hands, the very thing he knew would get under my skin. He was setting his agenda, letting me know that he was planning on doing what he pleased.

I was the leader in the classroom, however, and I made the decisions. I told him to return to his desk, gave him an official warning, and told him that if he chose not to follow my directions, he would miss the first half of the lesson. My tone was calm, though not friendly. I like to affect an attitude of ambivalence when a student breaks a classroom rule. Emotionally, I don't let it affect me in the least. I let the consequences do their job and don't make personal judgments or give lectures. Accountability works best if you don't interfere with it.

> *Whenever students act like this, especially in a dramatic way, I like to slow things down.*

Allen headed back toward his desk but threw a tongue depressor against the wall in protest. I didn't react at first, and I didn't take Allen's behavior personally. I knew this was his normal routine in trying to assert control and dominance. Whenever students act like this, especially in a dramatic way, I like to slow things down. This underscores the absurdity of their actions and creates anticipation. They wonder what I will do in response. This works in my favor by putting me in control.

After a long pause, I told Allen that he would have to watch the first half of the lesson from a desk that was separated from the rest of the class. I also told him that if he picked up the tongue depressor, sat up straight, and listened respectfully, I would invite him to be part of the class midway through the lesson. If he chose not to follow the instructions I gave him, I told him that he would miss the entire lesson. I had planned an engaging lesson and knew the students were going to have a great time. I couldn't wait to begin and show Allen what he was missing.

Allen picked up the tongue depressor, placed it where it belonged, and sat down. He was angry, which didn't bother me at all. How he felt about it was irrelevant. He was allowed to be angry, but after a moment of sitting, he yelled out, "You can't make me stay here!"

I wasn't going to indulge him by addressing his comment. That would put him in control. After another long pause, I said in a quiet voice, "I'm sorry, Allen, but you will have to miss the entire lesson. If you choose not to sit quietly for the rest of the lesson, I will send a letter home to your parents explaining everything that happened today."

Given Allen's behavior, I was aware that there may not be much support from home, but that wasn't the point of the letter. The point was to hold him to a higher level of accountability. A letter that a student must hand deliver and have signed forces him to acknowledge his poor behavior and take responsibility for it. It can be a powerful consequence for a child to hand his parent or guardian a letter and ask for it to be signed.

> *Using time-out for a consequence is only effective if the offending student feels he or she is missing something.*

The student then spends every recess with me until the letter is returned.[†] Spending one recess or more with a student is worth the effort in the beginning of the relationship. Once you prove that you will follow through and hold your students accountable for all rule violations, the problems largely disappear.

Following Through

As Allen sat and watched, the class had great fun working in groups as they tried to build the tallest building out of just a few materials. I joked with them and told a funny story while they worked. Using time-out for a consequence is only effective if the offending student feels he or she is missing something. Allen sat quietly through half the lesson and then raised his hand. I walked over to him and said, "Yes, Allen?"

Very politely he asked, "May I please join a group?"

---

†   Taking recess away from students can be very effective, but *only* if you are willing to actively supervise them yourself.

"I'm sorry, Allen, I said that you would have to miss the entire lesson. If you follow our class rules, you can join us next week."

He then yelled, "That's not fair!"

I didn't respond to his comment, but I did say, "I'll give you a letter to take home after school. If it's not back to me tomorrow morning before school, you will miss your recess and every recess until it's returned."

Allen was adept at manipulating teachers. After sitting quietly through half the lesson, he assumed that if he were polite enough, I'd give in and allow him to join the class. That was his experience with teachers in the past. But giving in would have undermined my efforts to create a comfortable and trusting learning environment. Going back on my word would communicate to Allen and the rest of the students that I couldn't be trusted. This creates stress and uncertainty that never fully leaves the classroom. Trust between the teacher and his or her students is crucial, and you won't have it if you don't mean what you say.

> *Going back on my word would communicate to Allen and the rest of the students that I couldn't be trusted.*

At the end of the school day, I dismissed my students a minute early so I could position myself outside Allen's classroom before he came out. I gave him his letter and reminded him that I wanted it signed and returned in the morning. I turned and headed toward the front office before he could begin to argue.

Arguing with students is never a good idea. I often see teachers arguing with students, but nothing good ever comes of it. There shouldn't be any negotiation regarding the rules and consequences of your classroom. For every time you bend your rules, you sow the seeds for multiple problems in the future.

As I was walking to the office, I noticed Allen's mother pulling up to the curb to pick him up. I had the time to walk out and talk with her, but doing so would have lessened the effect of Allen doing it himself. Teachers had been calling her for years, and she was well aware of his problems at school. I wanted Allen to be faced with a choice: decide to follow the rules and expectations of the class and have the letter signed or take a chance and see if Mr. Linsin really meant what he said. I was hopeful that he would bring the letter back the next morning, but I didn't expect it.

I was prepared to carry out the consequences to the end because I cared for Allen. I wanted to help him change his behavior for the better and improve his character—a great benefit for everyone involved but especially for him. To do this, I needed to hold him to a standard of behavior that was required for success in school.

A Change In Behavior

The next morning, I waited for him outside of his classroom where the students lined up. I wanted him to know that he was a priority for me. When Allen arrived, he walked up to me and, while seeming contrite, said, "I forgot your letter."

I said, "Okay, I'll see you at recess." And I immediately turned and walked away.

I released my class a minute early for recess and was waiting for him when he walked out of his classroom. His teacher walked out after him and said, "Hi, Mr. Linsin. Is there anything I can do?"

"No, thank you," I said. "Allen and I have business to take care of."

I walked Allen out to a bench and told him to sit down. To his surprise, I sat down next to him and used the time to do some paperwork. I didn't say anything more to him, but soon he said to me, "I'm good at soccer."

I replied, "Allen, I'd love to talk to you about soccer some time, but you're not allowed to talk until recess is over." When recess ended, I walked him back to class, and as I did, we had a short but pleasant conversation about soccer.

> *Teachers will often browbeat a student into promising not to break rules, but these are mostly empty promises.*

As he walked into his classroom, he turned and said, "Bye, Mr. Linsin."

"Don't forget the letter, Allen."

The next morning arrived, and Allen still didn't have the letter. We spent another recess together, and again, we had a nice conversation walking back. This time I told him a little about the following week's art project and reminded him that he had to have the letter back and follow my rules in order to participate.

Early the next morning, I heard a knock on my door. I opened it to find Allen holding the signed letter out to me. He was proud of himself. He was smiling and appeared thrilled to please me. I took the letter and said evenly, "Thanks, Allen. I'm glad you're going to join us. We're going to have a great time Friday."

There was no reason to discuss the situation further or force any assurances from him. Teachers will often browbeat a student into promising not to break rules, but these are mostly empty promises. The student tells the teacher what he or she wants to hear to get out of the conversation. Actions speak louder than words is an apt cliché. Allen's return of the letter told me all I needed to know.

During the couple of days leading up to the next art rotation, Allen must have said hello to me ten times. Dour and unpleasant much of the time, from then on he was always friendly toward me. You might assume that my strict adherence to a few rules would make troublesome students dislike me, but I've found the opposite to be true; they trip over their feet trying to please me.

When dealing with challenging students, I follow a few guidelines:

I treat them respectfully—even kindly.

I don't criticize personally or lecture them.

I don't talk to them more than I do other students.

I don't hold a grudge.

I do exactly what I say I will do.

Few of them have ever been dealt with in this manner, and they appreciate it. It allows me to demand impeccable behavior without creating friction between us. Afterward, when they have fulfilled all of their obligations, I invite them back to be a part of the class with open arms. I am clear with all students, however, that our classroom is a special place, and anyone who upsets its harmony is not welcome.

I always said hello back to Allen but treated him like any other student. Due to his abrasive personality and poor behavior, Allen was rarely treated like everyone else. Too often he was either scolded or hugged excessively by his teacher; both of which I found patronizing. I wanted him to feel normal and not like the outcast he often was. I was reinforcing, in a very subtle way, that I expected the same from him as I did from all students.

During the next art lesson, Allen was not perfect, but vastly better. I gave him one warning during the first ten minutes, and he was fine thereafter. Other than an occasional warning, he was well be-haved during the art rotation for the rest of the year. Firmness and persistence early in the school year set the tone for our relationship and paid dividends for the rest of the year.

Encouragement Alone Doesn't Work

Unfortunately, this wasn't the case in his regular classroom. I would see him hanging on the railing outside his classroom while his teacher pleaded with him to come inside. He was a terror on the playground, but like clockwork, he would be out there every day. His teacher told me that she didn't want to take away his recess because he had so much energy, and she thought his behavior would get worse if he lost the privilege.

> *Allen held his classroom hostage with his behavior and kept them from learning much of the time.*

Allen held his classroom hostage with his behavior and kept them from learning much of the time. In response, the teacher tiptoed around him, gave him lots of space, and hoped that he wouldn't be too disruptive. She also kept him at a desk pushed up against the front wall of the room, separated indefinitely from his classmates.

I guess one day she had had enough because the assistant princi-pal approached me and asked if I'd be willing to attend a meeting about Allen. The counselor, psychologist, his teacher, and mother were going to be there, along with the administrative staff. I agreed to attend and a few days later found myself sitting in the back of a conference room. I was mildly surprised to find Allen there. He sat in a chair with a scowl on his face, staring at the floor.

The meeting started well enough, with his teacher running down a list of his transgressions. His mother did the same, and then the principal asked Allen several questions. All were a variation of, "Allen, why do you think you're behaving badly?" For the most part he was non-communicative except for a few mumbled "I don't know's." There was no particular agenda to the meeting, and soon I was wondering why we were there.

After a moment of awkward silence, the counselor said, "We know you can do it, Allen. You're so smart." This opened the floodgates. While his teacher rubbed his shoulders, the rest of the group continued in this hollow vein for several minutes.

"Allen, we know you're capable of being a good boy."

"You know what you have to do, Allen, and we're here for you."

"You can do it, Allen."

"You know you can always come talk to me when you're angry, Allen."

"We are here to support you, Allen."

"You're so smart, Allen."

By this time, Allen was sobbing quietly. While everyone leaned toward him and cooed encouragement, I sat back with my legs and arms crossed in the universal body language position of, "I don't agree with what's going on here." At one point, the principal asked me what I thought. The group turned toward me and I said, "I think we should hold Allen accountable for his behavior." The group looked at me quizzically, as if to say, "That goes without saying. We're already doing that." Clearly, my definition of accountability was different than theirs.

We were wasting time cajoling him. What we needed to do was help his teacher design a set of clear rules and expectations for her classroom, as well as non-negotiable consequences if those rules aren't followed.

After getting Allen to concede that he would try to do better—whatever that meant—the meeting came to a close. As he rose from his chair, he looked at me and we shared a brief moment. His sheepish expression revealed his embarrassment over the faux tears he had shed. I shook my head as he averted his glance and walked out of the room.

There were smiles all around from the adults, but predictably, within a few days, Allen and his teacher were back where they started.

Children Want Accountability

We are failing children like Allen when we don't hold them accountable. Deep down, students like Allen crave accountability. His poor behavior screams out his desire for it. You can see the relief on his face when he walks into my classroom because he knows exactly what is expected of him. He knows where the boundaries are and what will happen if he ventures beyond those boundaries. He also appreciates, as all students do, the wonderful feeling of freedom that exists within those boundaries. It's comforting for them to know that there will never be a time when they're subject to the whims or moods of the teacher. It's a secure world that makes sense.

> *Deep down, students like Allen crave accountability. His poor behavior screams out his desire for it.*

Have you ever walked into a classroom and felt tension in the air? Some classrooms feel this way all the time—rooms where the boundary lines for behavior are undefined. The students don't know what to expect from one day to the next. Some days the lines might be closing tightly around them and other days they may be nonexistent, depending on the mood of the teacher.

Some teachers don't like posting rules and holding students accountable because rules seem too threatening, and they fear that they themselves might be perceived as harsh or mean.

In fact, the opposite is true. The unaccountable classroom is where teachers use sarcasm, putdowns, or yelling to gain control. Classrooms without clear rules and consequences tend to be dictatorial and are grossly unfair to children. Add a student like Allen to the mix, and you have the potential for a serious disruption in learning. A teacher with a fair discipline plan that holds students accountable never feels the need to use such hurtful methods and is able to maintain his or her equanimity in every situation.

> *The unaccountable classroom is where teachers use sarcasm, putdowns, or yelling to gain control.*

Accountability Is Good For Children

Today, children appear less inclined to take responsibility for their actions than ever before. They are quick to blame others and readily excuse their poor behavior, but guess what? It's not their fault. It's the adults around them who, for reasons such as preserving self-esteem, desiring to be their friend, or poor leadership, fail to teach them the valuable and lifelong lessons derived from demanding accountability.

Taking responsibility for the good and bad in one's life lowers stress, improves self-esteem, and humbles in the best and most endearing way. It builds character and integrity and promotes honesty and empathy for others. But these characteristics are rarely innate. It takes a strong leader willing to make the proper decision to hold students accountable for their behavior choices.

Accountability works and is good for children. Combined with exciting lessons and a self-assured teacher, the results are happy students and a stress-free learning environment.

A note about behavior management and test scores:

Many politicians and educational leaders insist on chasing the latest trends and experimental programs in education, at enormous cost to taxpayers, in hopes of finding the key to higher achievement and better test scores. But none of these measures will work unless there is a commitment to effective behavior management.

Students of teachers who are highly skilled at managing behavior will always do better and have higher test scores simply because they are more receptive to learning, experience fewer interruptions, and are on task for a larger portion of the school day.

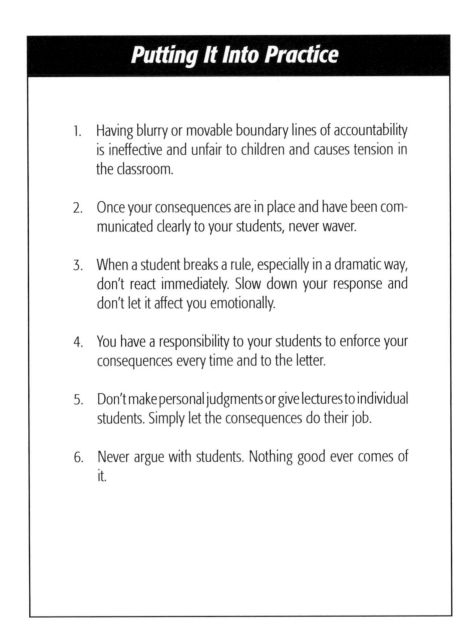

Putting It Into Practice

1. Having blurry or movable boundary lines of accountability is ineffective and unfair to children and causes tension in the classroom.

2. Once your consequences are in place and have been communicated clearly to your students, never waver.

3. When a student breaks a rule, especially in a dramatic way, don't react immediately. Slow down your response and don't let it affect you emotionally.

4. You have a responsibility to your students to enforce your consequences every time and to the letter.

5. Don't make personal judgments or give lectures to individual students. Simply let the consequences do their job.

6. Never argue with students. Nothing good ever comes of it.

Dream Class

Allow Freedom Within Boundaries

Show Them How

Build Rapport

Give Worthy Praise

Cultivate Independence

Transform Limiting Beliefs

Take Responsibility

Hold Students Accountable

Be A Great Storyteller

Help Shy Students Flourish

Treat The Cause, Not The Symptoms

Involve And Utilize Parents

Develop Maturity

Free Your Room, Free Your Mind

See The Best In Your Students

One Last Thing

Stories are the single most powerful weapon in a leader's arsenal.

—Howard Gardner

Key #9

Be A Great Storyteller

Everyone loves to hear a good story, but I like to tell one even better. Nothing I've ever done as a teacher has generated more response from students than when I tell a story. Much like reading, listening to a story can transport students to another time and place, but when the storyteller is sitting in front of them and giving a firsthand account of a rollicking adventure or a mysterious new friend, the experience can be much more powerful. I want to reach students any way I can, and I've found storytelling to be unrivaled in its power to get kids excited about school.

I like to tell stories about things that have happened in my own life. Only, I add a bit of suspense or maybe something supernatural. I first started telling stories about my childhood escapades, and now I'll tell stories about practically anything. When I tell a story, I like to have it mapped out in my head but not memorized. A story shouldn't sound practiced. I want my students to believe they are hearing it told for the first time.

Finding Good Stories

I'm always on the lookout for a good story. If I encounter something unusual or witness an event out of the ordinary, or even if a common occurrence sparks my creativity, I'll observe carefully and then turn the experience into a story. I'll give you a recent example. I was at a dinner party and found myself seated next to a man I had never met. We shook hands and introduced ourselves. I asked him what he did for a living, and we had a conversation covering topics ranging from sports to politics. He was tall and well dressed, with perfect hair parted neatly to one side. As I was listening to him, a quick thought flashed through my mind: he looks like a superhero.

> *As I was listening to him, a quick thought flashed through my mind: he looks like a superhero.*

A Mysterious Friend

At the end of the evening, another friend and I were talking with him when he mentioned that he was a runner. The two of us run with a group of friends every Saturday morning, so we asked him if he wanted to join us. He agreed and we've been friends ever since. So how does this make a good story?

Well, if I reveal to my students, through a series of stories told over two weeks, that this friend's name is Bruce and that he is reluctant to talk about his occupation—other than to say he works in law enforcement—then the story gets very interesting. One of the secrets of good storytelling is to include enough realism so that your listeners have trouble distinguishing fact from fiction. Here is a transcript of the story I told my students about Bruce.

> *The story with my new friend Bruce is getting stranger. I hope you can help me try to unwrap this mystery. A few unusual*

things happened when we ran together for the first time on Saturday. When I'm finished telling the story, I want to know what you think.

I was running a little late when I pulled up to the curb in front of the high school. My friends and I like to run in the football stadium. This particular stadium has tall grandstands on either side of the field where people sit to watch games. I counted the cars parked around me and recognized all of them as belonging to my friends. I was a bit disappointed because Bruce hadn't arrived yet, and I thought maybe he wasn't going to show up. I walked into the stadium through a large gate and noticed my four running buddies already in the process of warming up. I, too, began warming up, but as quickly as I could because we were starting soon.

We like to run on a red rubber track that encircles the field; it's soft and we can measure how far we run. Each lap represents about a quarter of a mile. I did a few push-ups and sit-ups to complete my warm-up, and then we began our run. Just as we were finishing our first lap, I saw Bruce running toward us. He was wearing black Nike running shoes with yellow trim and a black sweat suit with a thin yellow stripe along the sides. As it was the other night, his hair was perfect. He apologized for being late and then joined in the conversation. As he ran, he appeared to almost float above the ground. I could tell he was in excellent shape.

We ran for about 40 minutes, which didn't seem to be a great challenge for Bruce. He was very talkative, even when we sped up for our last couple of laps. When we finished, we sat down in a small rectangular area in front of the grandstand. There were a few foldout chairs scattered about and two small—about two feet tall—concrete cubes that were positioned closest to the wall that borders the first row of seats. I sat on one and Bruce on the other. The rest of the group sat in the chairs. We were joking and laughing as we rehydrated with water. Bruce was drinking an odd-looking sports drink called Radar Fuel. It was greenish in color, but when the sunlight met the surface of the liquid, I could see swirls of oily blues, yellows, and reds. I asked him if I could try it, but when I did, he quickly finished it and said, "I'm sorry. I was really thirsty."

I was wiping my face with a towel as we talked. It was a hot day and we were all sweating, but when I looked over at Bruce, he was as dry as he was before the run. He didn't look like he was sweating at all. After we cooled down, we stood and began to walk toward the gate that led out of the stadium. That's when I heard my friend Marc yell, "Look out!"

I ducked and started to get down on the ground. As I did, I glanced upward and noticed a bright red shape falling from the sky. Splat! The shape exploded on the ground and water spattered everywhere. It was a water balloon. Just then, another balloon, this one yellow, was heading toward us. And then another. And another. Soon dozens of water balloons of all different sizes and colors were bursting around us. They were coming from the other side of the grandstand.

We relaxed a bit when we discovered that the flying shapes were only water balloons, and Marc commented that it might be his young nephews playing a trick on us. It was then that I heard something strange. At least, I think I heard something. Very faintly, I'm almost sure that I heard a weird, high-pitched giggling, like a cackle a circus clown might make. After the flying balloons stopped, we headed for the exit. We were smiling and enjoying each other's company, but when I looked over at Bruce, I noticed that he had a look of concern on his face.

We continued walking out of the stadium and toward our cars parked in the street. That's when I saw a long, black limousine parked directly in front of us. There was a wrinkled old man leaning against it. When he saw Bruce, he hopped around to the back door and opened it with a flourish. Bruce looked a little embarrassed, but then he turned and, with a smile and a wave, said goodbye. I stepped toward my car, and as I slid the key into the door, I heard the old man say, "Your car, Mr. Wayne." And then Bruce replied, "Thank you, Alfred."

Telling A Story

Teachers make great storytellers. The practice we get from reading aloud great works of literature makes us naturals. There are several elements to telling a story that will help capture your students' attention and spark their imaginations.

First, a good story needs to be told with feeling. I like to think of storytelling as a dramatic performance. I visualize myself experiencing the story as it unfolds and try to capture how I would feel if it were actually happening. When making the faint giggling sounds, for example, I stand just outside the room so the students can experience the moment as if they were there. And when Bruce is leaving the stadium after the incident with the water balloons, I mimic his concerned expression juxtaposed against the smiling faces of the rest of the characters. I want the students to follow me in their imaginations from the moment I pull up in my car to the final moment when Bruce enters the limousine.

> *Teachers make great storytellers. The practice we get from reading aloud great works of literature makes us naturals.*

Second, good stories evoke vivid mental pictures. Using detailed descriptions of the setting and characters helps to create a visual image in the listener's mind, further drawing them deeper into the story. Small details, like the thin pinstripe running along the side of Bruce's pant leg and the color of the water balloons, intensify the experience for the listener. Athletes often use visualization to improve their performance because it allows them to react to the visualized images emotionally, as if they are actually experiencing them. When telling a story, I want to create a similarly visceral reaction in my students.

Third, good stories leave clues to help the listener draw conclusions.

A story with hidden meaning is much more interesting than one without. These clues, some subtle and some more obvious, prompt the listener into making predictions. Did you notice all of the clues pointing to Bruce's secret identity?

> *Bruce's reluctance to talk about his job*
>
> *Black and yellow warm-up suit*
>
> *Radar Fuel*
>
> *Bruce's lack of perspiration*
>
> *The high-pitched giggling*
> *(The Joker giggles this way)*
>
> *Bruce's concern over a silly prank*
>
> *Black limousine*
> *(Bruce is wealthy)*
>
> *His butler's name is Alfred*
>
> *Alfred called him "Mr. Wayne"*
> *(Batman's alias is Bruce Wayne)*

Sharing And Discussion

When telling stories with embedded clues, I can see gradual recognition in my students' faces as more and more of the clues are unearthed. When I'm finished, they can't wait to share their discoveries and conclusions. A hint of dramatic irony is used in this story to great effect. I never let on that I believe Bruce is anything more than a mysterious friend, and I don't display any understanding of the clues. When the students realize that they see something in the story hidden to the storyteller, in this case the true identity of Bruce, their faces light up with excitement. They love the idea that they know Bruce's secret before their teacher does.

I told this story in four parts (this was number two). After each part, I let the students discuss their thoughts with each other in small circles. They then select a representative to share their conclusions with me. At first I show reluctance to believe that my new friend is a superhero, but by the end of the fourth part, the evidence becomes so overwhelming that I have to concede that it might be true. The climactic moment arrives as this realization comes over me. The students are watching me silently as I feign contemplation, and then my eyes go wide as I yell, "Oh my gosh! I'm friends with Batman!"

> *The students are watching me silently as I feign contemplation, and then my eyes go wide as I yell, "Oh my gosh! I'm friends with Batman!"*

Surprisingly, few students ask me if the story is true. It's more fun to think of the possibilities of a real Batman than to ruin it with reality. It's implied, and at times even stated, that the veracity of my stories can't be trusted.

Storytelling For Beginners

Start With Short Anecdotes

If you haven't utilized storytelling in the past, start with short, three to five minute anecdotes. Draw on childhood stories in the beginning. They're easy for students to relate to, and you probably have many stored away in your memory. There is no reason for excessive preparation. If you have a story in mind, run through it mentally a couple of times on your drive to school in the morning, and then go for it.

Tell Simple Stories

Children are the best audience in the world. They are incredibly forgiving and are captivated by anything out of the ordinary or by things they are unfamiliar with. Your stories don't have to be elaborate to be effective. A simple, linear story will do.

For example, I recently told a story about how I gave a toast at a wedding. In the story, after getting everyone's attention by clinking my sparkling water glass with a spoon, I forgot what I was going to say. I acted out the awkward moment, and the students giggled throughout my stammering.

The story was nothing special, but because the subject was unfamiliar, they were fascinated by it. They wanted to know more about giving toasts and asked if I would show them how. So one day during lunch, we practiced. It was great fun, and now we give toasts frequently in class while holding up our water bottles.

"I would like to propose a toast. Here's to Monica, who scored the winning goal at recess today. Cheers!"

Use Them When Starting A New Unit

If you have trouble coming up with ideas, try telling stories that segue into units of study, or use them to introduce lessons. I once told a five-part story about the famed Egyptologist Howard Carter. I was teaching sixth grade, and to introduce our study of ancient Egypt, I told the tale of his 1922 discovery of King Tutankhamun.

After I finished, every student could accurately retell the story from memory, including details of the mummification process and what life was like in Egypt more than 3000 years ago. Taught separately, many students have trouble connecting with historical concepts, but in the context of an Indiana Jones-like adventure, they become enthralling and meaningful.

Be Yourself

Storytelling will come naturally if you stay true to yourself. No one can be you as well as you can, and your uniqueness is an asset when telling stories. You don't need to be an actor or be able to do impressions to be a great storyteller. Your authenticity is what will make your stories resonate with students.

Make Storytelling A Priority

Although storytelling itself isn't part of the regular curriculum, the impact it has on students warrants making it a priority, at least for a couple of days a week. It's certainly possible to choose themes for your stories that match those being taught in your subject area(s). But the main purpose of storytelling is its remarkable effectiveness in getting kids excited about school and thrilled to be a member of your classroom.

I want my students to feel like they can't wait to get to school in the morning. Storytelling can provide that little extra incentive, that missing piece of the puzzle that will infuse in your students the kind of passion and enthusiasm for school and learning that we all seek and treasure.

Putting It Into Practice

1. Children are mesmerized by great storytelling.

2. Storytelling is a strong motivator and can play an important role in getting children excited about school.

3. Storytelling is one of the true joys of teaching. With practice, anyone can do it well.

4. Always be on the lookout for stories. Keep a notebook handy, and when you notice something unusual or interesting, observe closely and take notes.

5. Add mystery or a touch of supernatural to make ordinary stories extraordinary.

6. Think of storytelling as a dramatic performance. Create an air of excitement and act out your story with feeling and emotion. Also, include small details and vivid imagery.

7. Leave clues that will help your listeners draw conclusions.

Dream Class

Allow Freedom Within Boundaries

Show Them How

Build Rapport

Give Worthy Praise

Cultivate Independence

Transform Limiting Beliefs

Take Responsibility

Hold Students Accountable

Be A Great Storyteller

Help Shy Students Flourish

Treat The Cause, Not The Symptoms

Involve And Utilize Parents

Develop Maturity

Free Your Room, Free Your Mind

See The Best In Your Students

One Last Thing

Our doubts are traitors,
and make us lose the good
we oft might win,
by fearing to attempt.

—William Shakespeare

Key #10

Help Shy Students Flourish

When I was ten years old, my father became friends with a NFL football player. At the time, sports were an all-encompassing hobby for me. I lived and breathed football, so when this local hero began showing up in my home, I was ecstatic. He invited me into the team locker room after games, and I would wander around and chat with my favorite players. I got to go to practices and play catch on the stadium field. It was a great experience, but I increasingly became uncomfortable around him.

As a boy, whenever I found myself in situations that were new or that I perceived to be socially threatening, I would retreat within myself. I would become self-conscious and could feel my legs shaking as I tried to engage in the most benign social interactions. Like the estimated 40% of children who occupy our classrooms, I had a shy personality.

Shy reactions are involuntary and are sometimes hard for others to understand. Shyness can come off as indifference or even arrogance, but it's nothing of the kind. Shy children tend to be empathetic, good listeners, and trusted friends, but these attributes can be lost on others—at least initially.

A Frustrating Cycle

After games I would congratulate this NFL player on his play and try to be myself, but feelings of heightened self-consciousness would envelop me. He could sense my discomfort because, in an effort to make me more comfortable, he became overly familiar and gregarious. Backslapping and telling jokes were his way of loosening me up, as were winks and playful roughhousing.

> *Unfortunately, the more you focus on a student's shyness and the more you try to draw the student out, the harder it is for the student.*

He worked hard to draw me out of my shell. He was a great guy, no doubt about it. But for someone who is shy, a person like him can be difficult to be around. Our interactions became a frustrating cycle. The more he would try to draw me out, the more I retreated back in and the worse I would feel about myself.

Shyness Affects Learning And Teamwork

It's like this with most shy children, and many well-meaning teachers react the same way as the football player. This is a normal reaction from a caring person. Unfortunately, the more you focus on a student's shyness and the more you try to draw the student out, the harder it is for the student. The result can be a group of students—an average of twelve in a class of thirty—who don't feel safe enough to fully participate and be active contributors.

It's so important to your students' academic and social development and to your success as a teacher that all of your students feel like they're contributing members of your class. Otherwise, you will never attain the strong sense of kinship that characterizes a dream classroom. Furthermore, a lack of participation inhibits learning and discourages teamwork. Understanding how to communicate with shy students is an often overlooked aspect of effective teaching.

Interacting With Shy Students

The best way to interact with shy students may seem counterintuitive at first, but in a short amount of time you will establish a relationship with each one that will allow them to flourish socially and academically.

Before a discussion about what you should do, it's important to establish what you shouldn't. Following these guidelines will enable your shy students to open up and be active members of your class.

Here Are A Few Things Not To Do:

◆Don't speak to shy students individually regarding their lack of participation, especially during the first few weeks of the school year. Talking to the teacher one-on-one, coupled with the added pressure of being asked to participate more, can be overwhelming. Asking for an individual conference with a student to discuss their shyness—or symptoms of their shyness—risks losing any progress made and increases the possibility of making it worse.

◆Don't recognize them in front of the class. You would think that recognizing shy students in front of their peers for something positive would boost their self-confidence and encourage participation. What it does is make them the center of attention, which for shy students can be nerve racking. It's perfectly fine to say simply, "Congratulations, Joanna. I heard you came in first place in the school-wide art contest. Way to go!" However, making a more formal announcement can be overwhelming for the student.

♦Don't mention their shyness. It surprises me how often I hear adults say to children, "Oh, you're so shy!" or "My daughter is very shy." Shyness can limit a child's learning, and we need to be careful not to label them as such. Have you ever felt pigeonholed by someone or labeled with a broad brush? It's a terrible feeling, and once a label is attached to you, it's difficult to overcome. It can make you second-guess the beliefs you have about yourself. Children are especially impressionable, and your words will have an effect. They often accept words from a person in authority, like a teacher, as fact. A student's shyness, even occasional, should never be labeled as such.

> A student's shyness, even occasional, should never be labeled as such.

♦Don't make more than a second or two of eye contact. Eye contact with students is important, but there is something about lingering eye contact that can bring about the characteristics of shyness in some students. When feeling self-conscious, children will have a harder time putting their thoughts together. Eye contact in small doses will give them a chance to collect their thoughts and then respond to you. Go ahead and make eye contact initially, and then look away to give them a chance to respond. Close your interaction with more eye contact.

♦Don't show any more interest in them than other students. Shy students are sensitive and extremely observant. They need time to come out of their shells and will do so if given room to breathe. In an effort to draw them out, some teachers may try to spend more time trying to get to know them. Initially, shy students are going to need more space. Certainly, it's not wise to ignore them, but let the student dictate the amount of interaction. I'm not suggesting that you don't talk with shy students or meet with them regarding their schoolwork as you would with any other student. What I'm advising is that you be patient in your efforts to get them more involved.

◆Don't allow a lull in conversation. When speaking to shy students, get to the point, get the information you need, and then move on. Dead time in conversation can make shy students self-conscious, which in turn will make them uncomfortable around you. Keep your conversations quick and direct.

◆Don't follow up if they participate. When shy students first start to participate in front of other students, you have them going in the right direction. They are becoming more comfortable with their surroundings. After they finish contributing, say to them briefly, "Good answer" or "I like that idea" and then move on. They're testing the waters. Let them play in the shallow end for a while. If you force them to expand their thinking, you risk drowning them. They probably practiced their answer silently for several minutes before deciding to participate. This was a big step for them, and you need to let them feel successful.

◆Don't make a big deal. This is sometimes hard for people to understand if they were not shy as a child. Demonstrative behavior, excess enthusiasm, or overreactions tend to make shy children very uncomfortable. "Wow, Jeffrey, you're playing on a baseball team? Awesome! Put er' there, buddy! Give me a high five!" A better way to handle it would be to say casually, "That's cool, Jeffrey. I like baseball too. Let me know how your season goes." This shows Jeffrey you're interested and gives him an opening to approach you in the future. And they always do.

◆Don't be too familiar. Most teachers are comfortable in their interactions with all children. With shy students, teachers have to be careful not to be too comfortable. It takes a while longer for a shy student to feel relaxed enough in his or her interactions with you before conversations can take on a familiar tone. Like all students, shy children enjoy the banter and back and forth with their teacher. It just takes a little longer to get there.

To encourage shy students to participate and to help them feel more relaxed around you and their new classroom, here are some ideas that work well.

Do The Following:

◆Keep conversations with shy students moving. When talking with you, they desperately want to have a normal conversation without long pauses or awkwardness. You can help by controlling the ebb and flow of the conversation. Keep it moving. Every successful conversation will bring them closer to being comfortable with you.

> *A teacher who tries to force more involvement from a shy student will cause the opposite reaction.*

◆Randomly call on them. Rick Morris, who is an acclaimed teacher and author, advocates calling on students randomly. His idea of using a deck of playing cards with a different name written on each card keeps all students on their toes and ensures that you're getting everyone involved. This is a great system for shy students. They know they're being called on because their name came up and not because the teacher wants to get them more involved. A teacher who tries to force more involvement from a shy student will cause the opposite reaction.

◆Accept them for who they are. Of course you don't want any of your students to feel uncomfortable, but sometimes you just have to let them be shy for a while. I can remember being hammered by a teacher in elementary school who would not accept my quiet nature. On the other hand, I have great memories of my fifth-grade teacher because she made me feel so comfortable in the classroom. She gave me time to adjust to my new environment, and she let me be myself.

◆Always behave in such a way that demonstrates to your students that their interactions with you are acceptable and normal. If a student is showing symptoms of shyness—shallow breaths, nervousness, losing their train of thought—pretend you don't notice. Pretend that you got the exact information you needed. After every conversation with you, your students should feel like they were successful. You are helping them to not only have a smooth back and forth conversation with you, but you're giving them confidence to have successful conversations with others.

> *After every conversation with you, your students should feel like they were successful.*

◆Talk to parents if you see signs of anxiety. Shyness is a normal reaction for some students when encountering anything new. However, if you follow the advice given here, and after a few weeks have a student who is still not showing his or her personality, then it might be time to have a conversation with the child's parents. Continued anxiety in a student may be a sign of something else going on, and parents should be informed.

A Knowing Teacher

Some years ago, I went to a wedding and ran into the fifth-grade teacher who I admired so much. I hadn't seen her since leaving elementary school. As soon as I saw her, I had this wonderful feeling of warmness. She recognized me immediately and gave me a hug. I felt the same comfort around her as I had when I was a kid. It had been 20 years or more, but I felt as if I could tell her anything. My friend who was with me at the time felt the same way. As we walked away, he summed up my exact thoughts with a pithy, "She's awesome."

A couple of years ago, my parents hosted a dinner party, and one of the guests was the football player who was so generous with me.

When my mom told me he was going to be there, the old feelings of shyness came rushing back. I hadn't seen him in many years. At first I worried about how I would react when I was around him, but then I thought, I'm a grown man, for gosh sakes. I'm being ridiculous. When he arrived at the party, I approached him immediately, and we had a good conversation. To be honest, I felt a bit of shyness when I first saw him, but it quickly passed.

As an adult, I'm able to overcome occasional shyness on my own. Children, however, often need the help of a knowing teacher to draw out their true personality. Doing so is not only a great benefit to the child but also to the teacher and to the rest of the class. A classroom where every student contributes improves learning for everyone.

Putting It Into Practice

1. An estimated 40% of children have shy personalities.

2. It's important to create an environment that allows all students to flourish socially and academically.

3. Knowing how to interact with shy students is an often overlooked aspect of effective teaching.

3. Students with shy personalities must feel safe in your classroom before they will become active, participating members.

4. Following the Dos and Don'ts guidelines will improve, and often eliminate, shyness behaviors.

Dream Class

Allow Freedom Within Boundaries

Show Them How

Build Rapport

Give Worthy Praise

Cultivate Independence

Transform Limiting Beliefs

Take Responsibility

Hold Students Accountable

Be A Great Storyteller

Help Shy Students Flourish

Treat The Cause, Not The Symptoms

Involve And Utilize Parents

Develop Maturity

Free Your Room, Free Your Mind

See The Best In Your Students

One Last Thing

Anything's possible if you've got enough nerve.

—J.K. Rowling

Key #11

Treat the Cause, Not the Symptoms

I know a teacher who insists that four of his students, all boys, be separated from each other throughout the school day because they have difficulty getting along. When his class lines up to leave the room, these four may not stand next to each other. If the teacher takes his class to the restroom, they may only go in one at a time. He has them sitting in opposite corners of his classroom, and whenever he drops them off with the music or art teacher, he asks these teachers to keep them apart.

I once witnessed the aftereffects of a pushing incident in the restroom. Evidently, two of the four found themselves in the restroom together and got into a shoving match while washing their hands. When the teacher found out, he reacted angrily, visibly showing his displeasure with a loud sigh, crossed arms, and a few harrumphs. Oddly, when he began to speak about the incident, he never mentioned the students' lack of control, their disrespect for each other, or that they used their hands with intent to harm.

He was angry with them because they were in the restroom together. He said, "How many times do I have to tell you? You're not allowed to be around each other. Not in line, not at recess, and not in the restroom. Stay away from each other!"

Besides reacting emotionally and not enforcing his expectations with any consequences—displaying poor teaching skills—the target of his anger was completely misplaced. He was upset because they were together. This incident happened in November. He planned to keep the four students apart for the rest of the school year.

> *But the problem was still there, and avoiding its symptoms isn't really teaching. It's more akin to babysitting, and it leads to headaches for the teacher and heartache for the students.*

Sadly, by being kept apart, the four students were learning an unintentional but harmful lesson from their teacher. In effect, the teacher was saying, "I don't believe you're capable of getting along with people who are different from you, so you should stay away from them." That was the "take away" for those boys.

The fundamental problem was that the four boys had difficulty getting along. The teacher chose to treat this problem by trying to avoid its symptoms—pushing, shoving, arguing, and the like. But the problem was still there, and avoiding its symptoms isn't really teaching. It's more akin to babysitting, and it leads to headaches for the teacher and heartache for the students.

Treating Symptoms With Avoidance

This same theme of treating the symptoms of chronic behavior problems with avoidance is played out much too often among teachers:

Brittany isn't allowed to play soccer because she gets upset and throws a tantrum if she loses.

Tony has to sit at an isolated desk every day because he can't control himself.

My class isn't allowed to wander around the library to look for books on their own anymore because they get too loud.

I only pair Sonja with students who will tolerate her because she doesn't work well with others.

We're closing the monkey bars because the students aren't using them safely.

David must stay away from certain students because he reacts angrily if they make fun of him.

Not to be confused with the effective use of consequences, which are predetermined, specific, and limited in duration, these broad reactions are used in an effort to avoid the problems from recurring. This avoidance strategy, however, doesn't teach students anything. Moreover, these reactions punish them unnecessarily and send the message to students that they don't have the capacity to improve or change their behavior.

A Common And Costly Mistake

Treating chronic behavior with avoidance is a mistake I see teachers making often, and it's a big mistake. It's bad for kids and bad for teachers. Most unsettling, it's a mistake many teachers don't realize they're making. They may even feel that classroom management is one of their strengths, confident in their ability to curb unwanted behavior by staying one step ahead of the problem. But this method comes with a high cost: bitterness, frustration, and low self-worth among students and additional stress for the teacher.

Confront The Cause Head-On

The solution is to confront the cause of recurring behavior problems head-on by arming students with a set of tools (i.e., strategies) designed to help them cope and then thrive in previously unsuccessful situations. For example, to address the cause of Brittany's behavior while playing soccer, not only would you allow her to play, but you would encourage her to. Only, you would teach her how to behave when she's losing by giving her precise tools to rely on and then enforcing a consequence on the spot if she digresses. And every day you would encourage her anew.

> *These tools aren't worth much if they're not explained thoroughly, modeled, and practiced through role-playing.*

The idea is to provide a set of tools for your students to use when they find themselves in situations that trigger unwanted behavior. These tools can be designed for an individual, a group of students, or for an entire class. In the case of the four boys, they needed to learn how to be friends. A simple set of tools for this purpose might look something like this:

1. *Greet each other with a hello and a high five or fist bump.*
2. *Use kind words when speaking with each other.*
3. *Take turns talking and playing.*
4. *Get involved in organized recess games together.*

These tools aren't worth much if they're not explained thoroughly, modeled, and practiced through role-playing. Also, unlike how their teacher handled the pushing incident in the restroom, anytime a classroom or school rule is broken, a predetermined consequence must be administered. The four boys also need to know how to respond when their teacher isn't there and one of them deviates from the tools and breaks a classroom rule.

I tell my students that in case I don't see or hear unacceptable behavior—defined by classroom or school rules—they must let me know about it. If they wish they can tell me privately, but I must know in order to protect each student's safety and right to enjoy school. I call it my Freedom of Information Act. I have the freedom and, more importantly, the responsibility to know whenever a student breaks a rule. And so do you.

Reduce Tattling

Very recently, a boy from another classroom approached me during recess and said, "Mr. Linsin, Daniel (a classmate) keeps picking on me, but when I tell my teacher, she says that she doesn't want to hear about it. We're not allowed to tattle, but I don't know what else to do."

I addressed his problem and then thought about his teacher. I hear this complaint from teachers a lot, and I can understand it. They get tired of students telling on each other, and so they discourage it. But the reason some students tattle so frequently is because they're frustrated. They don't have the means to handle the problems themselves—however minor or petty—and too often, the teacher isn't always holding every student accountable.

In classrooms where rules are faithfully enforced and teachers are showing students how to handle recurring problems themselves, tattling is infrequent but still necessary. You can't possibly see or hear everything, and it's healthy for students to speak up for themselves. We should encourage our students to speak out against injustice and to stand up for what is right. But we have to show them how and when they can safely do it themselves and when they need to let a teacher know.

Tools For Common Playground Situations

If you are presenting tools to individual students, you may need to teach them during recess or before or after school. However, tools like those regarding friendship are valuable for all students, so you would probably want to teach them to the whole class during regular school hours. You may also want to teach your students tools for dealing with common playground situations. For example, if someone calls them a name or makes fun of them at recess, how should they respond?

> *"You may not talk to me that way. I deserve to be treated with respect!"*

In response to name calling, I teach my students how to look the offender in the eye and speak to them with confidence. Do they really do it? You bet, no problem. If you give your students the tools they need to successfully navigate their way through potentially troublesome situations, they will use them. You will find that your students will rarely make the wrong choice when caught in situations for which you have provided tools.

I teach these success tools to my students because they work. My students, in turn, revel in their newfound confidence. It's often funny to hear stories afterward. Someone will say something to one of my students like, "Valerie, your pants are too long. They're dragging on the ground. Gross!"

Valerie will throw her shoulders back, lift an index finger in the air and say dramatically, "You may not talk to me that way. I deserve to be treated with respect!" The storyteller will then recall the shocked face of the perpetrator who responds sheepishly, "Okay, I'm sorry."

These tools, whether used for losing a soccer game with grace, getting along with classmates, or responding to name calling, are incredibly powerful and will give your students more confidence and a stronger belief in their ability to overcome obstacles. And they're so much better than the alternative: handcuffing students through the weak-kneed and ineffective practice of avoidance.

Confronting the cause of chronic behavior problems works and is right for your students. Show them what to do and how to do it. Teach, model, role play, supervise, enforce, and encourage. Arm them with the tools they need to succeed, and you will see them thrive where once they failed.

Putting It Into Practice

1. Treating symptoms is exhausting and time-consuming and does nothing to help your students learn the skills necessary to be successful.

2. Treating symptoms damages self-esteem by communicating to your students that they are incapable of changing poor behaviors.

3. Confront the cause of behavior problems head-on by teaching your students the skills they need to handle challenging situations themselves.

4. Arm your students with specific tools they can rely on when confronted with situations that prompt their poor choices.

5. Supervise your students closely and monitor their progress.

6. Safety is paramount, and students need to know how and when they can safely handle situations themselves and when to tell the teacher. For example, bullying behavior would always be handled by a teacher.

Dream Class

Allow Freedom Within Boundaries

Show Them How

Build Rapport

Give Worthy Praise

Cultivate Independence

Transform Limiting Beliefs

Take Responsibility

Hold Students Accountable

Be A Great Storyteller

Help Shy Students Flourish

Treat The Cause, Not The Symptoms

Involve And Utilize Parents

Develop Maturity

Free Your Room, Free Your Mind

See The Best In Your Students

One Last Thing

Enthusiasm is everything.
It must be taut and vibrating
like a guitar string.

—*Pele*

Key #12

Involve And Utilize Parents

Recently, I had the opportunity to visit several classrooms during an open house event at a school near my home. The teachers appeared to have taken great care in preparing for the arrival of parents and families. The classrooms were clean and beautifully decorated, the teachers were dressed in their finest outfits, and a wide assortment of food and drinks were available in each classroom. Still, it was poorly attended.

Near the end of the evening, I entered a fifth-grade classroom and was met warmly by the teacher. She was eager to show me around despite my not being a parent. As I recorded my name on her sign-in sheet, I noticed that I was only her twelfth visitor. Eleven parents had shown up from a class of thirty-one students, and not one had signed up to volunteer in her classroom. "I'm so disappointed," she said to me. "I reminded the students over and over, and most said that their parents would be here. I don't know what happened."

The Benefits Of Parent Involvement

According to the National Parent Teacher Association, decades of research has shown that when parents are involved in their child's education, students have:

- ◆Higher grades, test scores, and graduation rates.
- ◆Better school attendance.
- ◆Increased motivation.
- ◆Better self-esteem.
- ◆Lower rates of suspension.
- ◆Decreased use of drugs and alcohol.
- ◆Fewer instances of violent behavior.

These benefits warrant making parental involvement a top priority. But they're not the only reason why involving parents is a key to creating your dream class. The other reason is that, when fully utilized, parents can help your classroom run more efficiently and allow your teaching to be more focused.

Why Do Some Teachers Attract More Parents?

I once taught at a school where 100% of parents belonged to the PTA. These were parents who were aware of the importance of being involved and were determined for their children to receive the best education. It was not uncommon for me to rotate a dozen or more parent volunteers through the classroom every week, and it was rare not to have every parent show up for open house. It was a wonderful environment to teach in and a luxury to have so many parents eager to get involved.

Most of my career, however, has been spent in schools where only a handful of parents make up the PTA and typically less than 50% attend open house. Very few parents volunteer to help in most classrooms.

But at these same schools you will find a few anomalies, classrooms where parents are teeming—irrespective of grade level. What are these teachers doing differently? How are they able to attract up to 100% parent attendance at school events while so many others struggle to draw even half? Why do they have a surplus of parents willing to help in their classrooms and others don't have any?

Techniques From A Sales Pro

My dad has been an independent sales representative his entire career. Nearing seventy now, he continues to work with the same energy as ever, with no plans to retire. And why should he? He is his own boss, goes on vacation when he chooses, and doesn't work long hours. Sounds like a great job, doesn't it? The fact is, working for commission can be brutally competitive, and only a small percentage of sales reps are especially successful. With my dad, however, it has become a foregone conclusion. Regardless of the economy, he is successful year after year.

Growing up, I was curious about what he did for a living because, unlike other dads, he was home a lot and could often be found talking on the phone with great enthusiasm. I've probably heard him talk to customers hundreds of times and have had the privilege of accompanying him on several sales calls. While observing him, I identified three steps he follows with every customer:

#1 He enthusiastically promotes his product.

#2 He boldly asks for sales.

#3 He delivers on his promises.

Many years ago, I began applying similar steps in my efforts to get more parents involved and was pleased with the results. In one year,

I went from having about a dozen parents attend open house to nearly every parent attending and went from one parent volunteer per week in my classroom to ten. After sharing these steps with other teachers, I'm convinced that anyone can repeat my success—with a lot less effort than you would imagine.

Step 1: Promote Your Product

It helps to think of your classroom as a thriving business and the parents of your students as your customers. Your product is the educational experience you've created for their children. Like any business, it's important to enthusiastically promote your product. If you aren't excited about what is happening in your classroom, no one else will be either. Parents will be attracted to your passion for the exciting learning taking place, and they'll want to be part of it—if you take the time to share with them and are exuberant in your message. Whenever you have an opportunity to speak with parents, even for a minute or two, explain some of the upcoming projects you have planned, and then invite them to join you.

> *It helps to think of your classroom as a thriving business and the parents of your students as your customers.*

Step 2: Boldly Ask

Often, in advance of open house or back-to-school night, school administrators will print up flyers for each teacher to pass out to students, giving the basic information of when and where. These are taken home stuffed in pockets and backpacks and hopefully find their way to the primary guardian. Parents get these same tired flyers, which are typically no more than reminders, every year. But these flyers don't come close to communicating the value and importance that needs to be placed on their attendance. This flyer-only approach will yield mediocre results every time.

If, on the other hand, a parent were to receive a special invitation from the teacher sealed in an envelope and addressed to them personally, there would likely be a different result. An example of such a letter, written simply and directly and proven to be effective, is located at the end of the chapter. A personal invitation like this can make a big difference. There can be no doubt that parents are not only welcome, but the implication is that they are even expected to attend.

> *It's okay to communi-cate to parents that, unless they have a prior committment, they need to be there.*

It's okay to communicate to parents that, unless they have a prior commitment, they need to be there. You should always be unfailingly polite and respectful, but be bold in asking for their attendance and support.

Including a RSVP makes your letter even more effective. By doing so, you will get far better attendance, and rarely will someone answer in the affirmative and not show up.

When the due date for the RSVP slip arrives, call any parent you didn't get a response from. Remind them of the importance of attending and how much you would like to see them there. Tell them that you need the RSVP form back the next day, even if they decide not to attend. Parents will be more likely to show up if they must check a box indicating whether they will be there or not. Few commitments are more important than attending their children's school events, and when asked to choose, most will opt to be there.

I know it's common for teachers to have their students write letters to parents inviting them to attend, and I think these letters can be helpful, especially as reminders on the day of the event. An additional letter from you, however, suggesting that they need to be there will prove most effective.

When the evening arrives and you get a large turnout, you must take advantage of it. I've noticed that many teachers leave a volunteer sign-up form located near the parent sign-in sheet. This seems like a good place for it, but to get as many volunteers as possible, you need to ask each parent personally.

Before you do, it's important to explain in your opening remarks exactly what they will be doing if they volunteer and how their volunteering will directly benefit the students. Later, when making your rounds and saying hello to parents, smile and, while holding out your sign-up form, confidently ask, "The students and I would love to have you volunteer to help in our classroom. Is there a day you would be available?"

Step 3: Deliver On Your Promise

Some parents are wary about volunteering because of their experiences helping in the past. Too often, they're asked to grade papers or perform menial tasks like cutting construction paper or stapling materials. Volunteering needs to be rewarding to them and beneficial to your class. They're taking time out of their day to come and help, and it's important that you deliver on your promise to make it worth their while.

I've found that the best way to utilize volunteers is to have them help during independent reading time. They sit with students one at a time for about ten minutes while the student reads to them. This is a great use of their time and an excellent way to keep track of your students' personal reading.

I provide each volunteer with a clipboard, a roster, and a form they fill out with each reader. The form consists of open-ended questions used to assess comprehension and determine if the book is the right level for the reader. We have a short meeting afterward where parents bring up concerns they have regarding any of the students.

A teacher may be able to read with every student individually once every couple of weeks, and I think it's important to (continue to) do so. But if you add several well-trained volunteers, you can cover the entire class in a couple of days. Checking in with students this often keeps them motivated and growing in their reading skills, and the only way to do it is with parent volunteers.

> *Another benefit to having parents help you in this way is that you only have to show them what to do and how to do it, once.*

I also like to use literature circles or social studies and science groups with parent volunteers. I've found parents to be an indispensable resource for helping to make these small groups run smoothly, allowing me to focus my efforts on student learning rather than whole class management. I personally rotate through each group while parents help facilitate the others. I encourage parents to be more like active observers than participants. As much as possible, the students lead the groups. The parent volunteers are there to help solve problems and keep students working toward their learning goals.

In my experience, parents love this type of work. They're involved in meaningful interactions with students and are able to apply their skills and life experiences to help them learn and improve. They're also able to see the impact their involvement has on their own children. I've had parents enjoy the experience so much that they continue to help in my classroom even after their own child moves on to the next grade level.

Another benefit to having parents help you in this way is that you only have to show them what to do and how to do it, once. They do the same thing every time they come in, so there is no need to interrupt the flow of the school day and no need for you to do any extra planning.

Non-English Speaking Parents

It's important to communicate to non-English speaking parents that you value them and the unique abilities they can bring to your classroom. Some may be reluctant to volunteer because they fear that the language difference may hinder their ability to help. Although you may have to be more creative, I don't find it difficult to get them involved in helping students.

Many times I've had Spanish-speaking parents lead groups consisting of students who also speak Spanish. The students read the material in English, but when it's time for discussion, they confer in Spanish. Given the importance of having parents involved, this is a small concession.

I had a parent volunteer in my classroom who spoke only Vietnamese. During independent reading time, I had her sit with my Vietnamese students one at a time as they read aloud to her in English. After they finished reading, they would summarize for her in Vietnamese, and then she would ask the comprehension questions—which I had translated. Her daughter would act as an interpreter for me whenever we spoke about how the students were progressing, and this system worked very well. The mother felt great about the work she was doing, her daughter was proud, and I had a reliable volunteer who really cared about the students.

Make Parents Feel Welcome

Several times I've overheard teachers asking parents to make an appointment before coming by to observe the class. I think this is a mistake. Requiring parents to make an appointment discourages them from getting involved. The formality of calling ahead and setting a time—like they're making a reservation at an upscale restaurant—can be intimidating for some parents and inconvenient for others. It also communicates, intentionally or not, that you're not terribly interested in having parents involved.

When a parent approaches you about visiting your classroom, a better response would be, "Come by anytime. We would love to have you. Here is a copy of our schedule." Parents who feel welcome are more likely to volunteer, more likely to attend school events, and more likely to take an active role in their child's education.

Parent Involvement Benefits All Students

Your reputation for offering parents an enjoyable volunteer experience will spread to other parents. I've had many parents approach me the first day of school and tell me how excited they are to work in the classroom. I'm honored when this happens and so appreciative to have the help.

In addition to the many benefits to their own children, parents can enhance the quality of the experience you offer to all of your students. But you have to be fervent in promoting your program, bold in asking for their participation, and determined to deliver on your promise to provide them with a meaningful experience.

Dear Mrs. Jones,   October 8, 2008

On Tuesday, October 16, our class is hosting Back-To-School Night from 5:30 – 6:30 in room B-8. We would be thrilled if you would be one of our honored guests. The students have worked hard to prepare the room for your arrival and have each made a special gift they look forward to presenting to you. The schedule will be as follows:

5:30 – 5:50 – Important Presentation For Parents

5:50 – 6:00 – Question And Answer Period

6:00 – 6:30 – Meet Mr. Linsin - Tour The Classroom - View Student Work

Your attendance at this important event is needed. Information will be given that is critical to the academic success of your child. I look forward to seeing you there. Please sign and detach the RSVP slip below and return it with your child to me no later than Thursday, October 12.

Thank you for your support of our classroom.

Best Regards,

Mr. Linsin

☐ I will be attending Back-To-School Night for room B-8.

☐ Due to a prior commitment, I will not be able to attend.

Signature_____

Putting It Into Practice

1. When fully utilized, parents can help your classroom run more efficiently and make your teaching more focused.

2. Enthusiastically promote your product to parents—which is the educational experience you have created for their children.

3. Send personal letters to parents inviting them to attend school or classroom events, and include a RSVP.

4. To get parent volunteers to help in your classroom, ask them personally.

5. Make volunteering rewarding to parents by having them work directly with students.

6. Be creative in getting non-English speaking parents involved in your classroom.

7. Always make parents feel welcome.

Dream Class

Allow Freedom Within Boundaries

Show Them How

Build Rapport

Give Worthy Praise

Cultivate Independence

Transform Limiting Beliefs

Take Responsibility

Hold Students Accountable

Be A Great Storyteller

Help Shy Students Flourish

Treat The Cause, Not The Symptoms

Involve And Utilize Parents

Develop Maturity

Free Your Room, Free Your Mind

See The Best In Your Students

One Last Thing

A mind that is stretched by a new experience can never go back to its old dimensions.

—Oliver Wendell Holmes

Key #13

Develop Maturity

Developing maturity in your students will make them more resilient, less self-centered, and better prepared to take on the many challenges that children and young people face. Mature students are also calmer, more open to learning, and make teaching more enjoyable and less stressful. And make no mistake, you can have a tremendous influence on its development.

Maturity levels among classrooms can vary wildly depending on the teacher—sometimes startlingly so. Students in one classroom may appear two years older than their grade level counterparts as a direct result of their teacher's style of interaction and willingness to place them in situations that will foster its growth.

Immature behavior can be greatly reduced, or even eliminated, and mature behavior developed by employing a few strategies.

Avoid Baby Talk

The way a teacher speaks to his or her students has a strong influence on maturity. Talking to students using baby talk is commonly heard in the primary grades, but it's a mistake, even for kindergarten teachers. Baby-talking teachers beget baby-talking students, who will behave at the level they speak. If the speech is immature, so too will be the behavior.

The term baby talk is an exaggeration that refers to a way of speaking that oversimplifies language and reinforces immaturity. Although employed differently than by primary teachers, this oversimplification of voice and speech can also be heard by teachers of upper elementary students and above.

> *Talking to students using baby talk is commonly heard in the primary grades, but it's a mistake, even for kindergarten teachers.*

I once taught across the hallway from a teacher who was often beside herself with stress. Although she worked hard to prepare engaging lessons and her students appeared happy to be in her classroom, they tended to be immature, almost baby-like. It was a first-grade class, but she was constantly tying shoes and helping kids on with their coats and sweaters.

Her students were needy and seemed to crave—even demand—her attention. They spoke in babyish voices, and when they experienced the slightest adversity, their first inclinations were to complain and desire to give up. It was a stressful environment to teach in, but it could have been improved considerably by making a few changes. Foremost among them would be changing the way she used her voice to communicate with her students.

Because of the proximity of our classrooms, I could often hear her as she addressed her students. She would excitedly elevate her vocal pitch above what is her normal speaking voice, slow her enunciation excessively, and deliver her messages in shortly clipped phrases. It reminded me (not too inaccurately) of how one might talk to a two-year-old or a brand new puppy.

> *It reminded me (not too inaccurately) of how one might talk to a two-year-old or a brand new puppy.*

Reflexively, her students responded in kind, both in the way they spoke and how they behaved. To make matters worse, her response to their immature behavior was often indulgent.

I haven't seen this teacher in several years, but I'm certain that if she were to change the way she used her voice, she would notice marked improvement in her students' maturity, and her stress level would decrease.

Although this is an extreme example, more subtle degrees of baby talk can be heard on most elementary school campuses, no matter the grade level.

I know a couple of excellent kindergarten teachers. Notably, both talk to their students as they would talk to a fellow teacher, with one exception. They use a more limited vocabulary. This doesn't mean that they only use words at the students' level of development. On the contrary, they often use words beyond a kindergarten level. Except, they make sure that their meaning is clear to the students—that context, situation, and nonverbal clues are strong enough to support any unfamiliar word or phrase. One thing you won't hear in their classrooms is baby talk.

You Are Not A Peer

When it comes to promoting maturity, guard against becoming too informal with your students. Steer clear of words and phrases that are popular with them. This tends to happen more often in middle and high school, but I see it on the elementary level as well. I shudder every time I hear a teacher say "my bad." Using slang in an attempt to build rapport doesn't work. It can't work. You are not a peer and shouldn't try to act like one.

> *The next time you find yourself in a disruptive situation, don't react immediately. Get the facts first, make a decision, and then calmly act.*

Seek your students' respect first and forget friendship. It's not in your interest or that of your students to be on equal footing with them, and it doesn't provide the model of maturity they need. There can be a certain level of friendship, but it is one born of a clearly understood student-teacher relationship. The line between the two should never blur.

Model Maturity

Another way to support the growth of maturity in your students is to model what it looks like. Keep calm in stressful situations. Show your passion during lessons or when you're motivating your class, but when an important activity goes awry or when a student misbehaves, react evenly. It keeps the level of negative energy down and establishes for your students how to behave when things don't go their way.

Immature students tend to overreact and become excitable. Show them how to react when something doesn't go well. Don't raise your voice or show your frustrations. When you do, you give license for your students to do the same. The next time you find yourself in a disruptive situation, don't react immediately. Get the facts first, make a decision, and then calmly act.

Give Students A Chance To Try

Independence is a characteristic of maturity and, as covered in a previous chapter, encouraging it in your students will improve their level of maturity. Allowing ample time for your students to solve their own problems and challenges before stepping in with clues or ideas is smart. Giving them chances to rely on themselves rather than looking to you can improve learning and raise confidence.

Never do for your students what they can do for themselves, and if you're not sure, give them a chance to try. You can do this without appearing callous by being honest. Say, "I'm happy to give you some suggestions, Laura, if you really need them, but I think you can handle this yourself. Why don't you give it a shot?"

This can be hard for some teachers; most of us are exceptionally considerate by nature. But if you can resist your inclination to step in and help, you'll discover your students tackling more challenging situations with boldness.

Students With Special Needs

I'm a proponent of having students with special needs enrolled in regular education classrooms—not so much because of the benefits to the child, which in most cases are many, but because of the opportunities it presents to the other students.

One year I was asked if I was interested in having a blind student in my sixth-grade class. Her name was Maria, and it would be her first time in a regular education classroom. She was blind from birth and was dependent on others for an assortment of everyday tasks. She was learning how to use a "white cane" and needed an escort whenever she left the classroom.

Maria had a demanding personality and could be hard on those assisting her, but she had a great sense of humor and a beautiful singing voice that endeared her to the other students. It was a new experience for everyone. I thought it provided a great opportunity for my students to learn important life lessons.

> *Seeing life from a different perspective is valuable, and through Maria my students were able to do that.*

Seeing life from a different perspective is valuable, and through Maria my students were able to do that. They witnessed her everyday struggles with simple tasks that they took for granted, and it helped bring out the best in them. The students who previously seemed only interested in themselves were the most profoundly changed.

Encourage Your Leaders To Buy-In

I remember noticing a boy named Arturo lingering around his desk every day after being dismissed to recess. At first I couldn't figure out what he was doing, but one day I kept my eye on him. Very subtly, he would glance in Maria's direction to make sure she had an escort for recess. Only when she was in safe hands would Arturo himself go out to recess.

Then came a day when her assigned escort was absent, and I had forgotten to assign a substitute. When recess came, I looked up and saw Arturo holding his elbow out for her to take. It was the first time I could recall ever seeing the two of them interact.

I got tears in my eyes watching them. Arturo was a tough kid who had been involved in his share of trouble, including minor brushes with the law. He was also a natural leader who was immensely popular with his peers. At recess that day, I watched him as he unabashedly helped Maria while she was swinging on a swing set. He made it cool to help others.

The other students noticed him walking Maria back to the classroom. They watched him intently but didn't say a word. His actions spoke volumes and did more for my goal of creating a spirit of togetherness, which is emblematic of class maturity, than anything I could do. Encourage students with the most influence to buy into your program, and others will follow.

> *When planning field trips, eschew the ordinary. They will have plenty of opportunities to go to the zoo.*

The same year there was a classroom of students with severe autism on our campus. I required seven of my students to help in their classroom two days a week, doing one-on-one tutoring. I rotated in a different group of students every few weeks, and everyone participated.

If you have an opportunity like this at your school, take advantage of it. Special education teachers are usually open to having other students help, and I think it's important in this age of selfishness to expose kids to people who are different or less fortunate than they are.

New Experiences

Immature students are preoccupied with their wants and feelings and have trouble seeing beyond their limited worldview. Exposure to unfamiliar places and experiences will open their eyes to new ways of seeing.

When planning field trips, eschew the ordinary. They will have plenty of opportunities to go to the zoo. If it's a place schoolchildren commonly frequent, go somewhere else. I realize that sometimes teachers are limited to trips that fit the curriculum, but be creative. It's possible to satisfy your obligations to grade level themes and standards and also expose your students to something novel.

I was teaching in an inner-city school and saw a flyer for a free field trip. The offer stated that if any number of certificated teachers were willing to go on a half-day training hike into California's San Gabriel Mountains, they would get a free bus to take their students on the same hike. It sounded fun, so I went.

The hike was breathtaking. There was no paved trail, which I loved, and it didn't require a guide. This meant that I could design the trip how I pleased. The hike was meant as an opportunity to perform science experiments in a natural environment. For example, you could stop along the way and test the water speed of an adjacent stream.

I took a poll in class and discovered that none of the students had seen snow before. Not one! So when I called to choose a date for our hike, I asked for January. The head of the outdoor education department said that his policy was not to schedule hikes in the winter months. But after some cajoling, he offered that it was possible. He tried hard to convince me that the trip was better in the early fall or late spring, but I was adamant. Eventually, he relented and soon we found ourselves piling out of a school bus and into a winter wonderland. It was glorious!

We hiked for miles, had snowball fights, and made snowmen. We didn't find time for experiments, but they seemed trivial when compared to this first-time experience. I felt blessed to be part of it. In one day, each student took a giant step beyond his or her previous understanding of the world. This should be your primary goal every time you take a field trip.

Seeing The World Differently Than Before

Sharing your life experiences with students is another way to expand their perspectives. Draw them away from their subjective view by telling stories and sharing pictures of memorable and life-changing events in your past. Put them in your shoes as you explain the experience of climbing into the pyramids of Egypt or of your first day of college. In my experience, students are mesmerized by such stories. After each one, they will see the world slightly different than before and inch ever closer to a more mature outlook and worldview.

When I was in high school, I heard Dave Winfield speak. He is a Hall of Fame baseball player. His speech resonated with me because he never mentioned sports. He said that for young people to grow in character, they should travel, read, and meet people different from themselves. In the years since, my pursuit of these goals has born out the truth of his advice.

To view the world beyond the confines of one's subjective experience has immense value. We can encourage an expanded view for our students by exposing them to people and experiences different from their own. By doing so, you will notice in them a growth in maturity that only comes from seeing outside the limits of their daily experience.

Putting It Into Practice

1. Mature students are calmer, less self-centered, more open to learning, and more prepared for future challenges.

2. Don't use baby talk or slang. It encourages immature behavior.

3. Model maturity by reacting evenly in all situations.

4. Pursue having students with special needs in your classroom. Their presence provides endless benefits to your classroom community.

5. Expose your students to unfamiliar places and experiences.

6. Share your life lessons and adventures through stories and pictures.

Dream Class

Allow Freedom Within Boundaries

Show Them How

Build Rapport

Give Worthy Praise

Cultivate Independence

Transform Limiting Beliefs

Take Responsibility

Hold Students Accountable

Be A Great Storyteller

Help Shy Students Flourish

Treat The Cause, Not The Symptoms

Involve And Utilize Parents

Develop Maturity

Free Your Room, Free Your Mind

See The Best In Your Students

One Last Thing

Organizing is the act of giving yourself more time and peace of mind.

—Peter Walsh

Key #14

Free Your Room, Free Your Mind

Early in my teaching career, our school morphed from a traditional-calendar school to a year-round school. The change was made because of overcrowding. Every classroom needed to be in constant use throughout the year, meaning that when teachers went on vacation, which was every three months, they needed to move out of their classrooms. When they came back from their one-month break, they moved into a new room.

Veteran teachers had an especially difficult time with this. Some had been in the same classroom for ten years or more and had accumulated a mountain of resources. The principal believed that a clutter-free working environment spawned better productivity, and he used the change to a year-round calendar as an opportunity to rid the school of unused equipment.

A dumpster was brought in to help reduce the massive amounts of obsolete material. The principal purchased a rolling cabinet for each teacher to put his or her supplies in. Upon leaving a classroom, the teacher would roll the cabinet into a large storage container located on campus.

> *One year a principal left a note on my desk that read, "A clean desk is a sign of a sick mind." On the back it said, "Actually, it's a sign of good teaching."*

Before moving out, the room had to be gutted of everything except the furniture. Even staples had to be removed from the walls. Everything else needed to fit into your rolling cabinet or be taken home. I quickly learned how to keep only those things I needed and to discard the rest. It was a great lesson. I kept my entire collection of teaching materials in six Xerox paper boxes.

A Sign Of Good Teaching

Years later, when I transferred to a school with a traditional calendar, I continued to limit my resources to what I could fit into those six boxes. I liked the unfettered feeling of not being weighed down by excess and how neat and tidy my room looked. I got compliments all the time, and I soon discovered that my limited supply of stuff, combined with an increasing proclivity for neatness, made me a more effective teacher.

One year a principal left a note on my desk that read, "A clean desk is a sign of a sick mind." On the back it said, "Actually, it's a sign of good teaching." I got a laugh out of it, but through experience knew it to be true—the back of the note, anyway. I'm sure there are exceptions, but I've never known an outstanding teacher who had a messy or cluttered classroom.

The Benefits Of An Uncluttered Classroom

There are so many benefits to keeping your room clean and orderly that I see it as one of the most important keys to creating your dream class. At the top of the list is that it can help you and your students think more clearly.

A cluttered workspace can clutter the mind as well. Clearing the non-essentials from your classroom will help you focus on your students and eliminate the distracting need to search for materials. It's nice to have everything you need at your fingertips. No more rooting around, emptying boxes and shelves in search of the one item you must have for your next lesson. You'll know where everything is and be able to access what you need quickly. You don't need to become as much of a minimalist as I am, but I think you'll find that you really don't need a lot of stuff to be a great teacher.

> *Keeping excessive amounts of teaching materials will lengthen your workday and add stress to your life.*

Keeping excessive amounts of teaching materials will lengthen your workday and add stress to your life. The decisions over what materials to use and the extra time spent looking for them create anxiety and remove you from those things that make teaching enjoyable. As much as you can, try minimizing the tasks you don't enjoy doing, and replace them with what you love about teaching—working with kids or creating exciting lessons and activities.

Clearing out your clutter will keep your teaching fresh. I know teachers who have multiple boxes labeled with particular months of the school year and have been relying on the same lessons, projects, and materials they contain for years. If you have an especially successful lesson, by all means keep samples and your notes from that lesson, but try limiting the information to what will fit into a simple file folder. And as much as possible, utilize the storing capacity of your computer.

Overstuffed Classrooms

I was scheduled to move into a new classroom one year and, as usual, had just a few boxes with me. It doesn't take me long to get ready for the first day of school, but I was excited to get started. I wanted to set up the furniture as I like it and begin covering the bulletin boards with a new color scheme.

When I approached the door of my new classroom, I noticed through the windows that the previous teacher was still working on removing her materials. She had a mountain of stuff. I considered dropping off my boxes and going to the school library to do some lesson planning, but I thought better of it and decided to help her. We were friends and I enjoyed her company, so I didn't mind lending a hand.

As soon as I began sifting through her materials, it became apparent to me that she didn't need more than half of it. She had samples of art projects she hadn't done in ten years, and I found basal readers from the 1980s! We laughed a lot as we tried to one up each other, looking for the most antiquated teaching tool. I would hold up a discovery with barely contained glee and say, "Do you think you'll be using this any time soon?" We must have thrown out a ton of unnecessary material.

Weeks later she was still saying to me, "I feel so much better now that I have room in my cabinets. I can actually find whatever I need."

It isn't just veteran teachers who have accumulated excessive materials and equipment. Scores of teachers with less than five years of experience have overstuffed classrooms, with equipment and boxes stacked on floors and atop cabinets. Undoubtedly, most of their students have similar habits.

Walk into a cluttered classroom and you will find dirty and messy desks. A major theme in this book is making your words congruent with your actions. How can you ask your students to keep their desks clean and orderly when you don't keep yours that way?

> *If you can eliminate the excess from your classroom and keep the top of your desk clear of clutter, you will lower your stress level and become a more efficient—ergo, more effective—teacher.*

If you can eliminate the excess from your classroom and keep the top of your desk clear of clutter, you will lower your stress level and become a more efficient—ergo, more effective—teacher. Moreover, a neat and appealing classroom environment communicates to all who enter, your commitment to lead a first-class educational experience for your students.

Beware Of The Gremlin

Once every couple of weeks, I'll draw an elfin-like character on the white board with a dialogue bubble over his head that reads something like, "Clean your desks, munchkins, or I will visit you tomorrow! Ha ha!" This means that the students have to clean out their desks, throw away old assignments, and organize, or the Gremlin will visit during the night and dump all of their things on the floor.

Now, I don't actually dump their stuff on the floor. What I do is choose a couple of students in secret and ask if they want to help me by placing their things on the floor in front of their desks before school the next day. Children love this kind of thing, and they always agree to help. The next morning, when the students arrive, they see that, sure enough, two of the desks had been emptied out and the contents dumped on the floor. One of the chosen students would say something like, "I guess I didn't clean it well enough. Next time I'll know better."

Everyone gets a good laugh out of it, and then we go about our business. You can certainly have the students clean their desks every week or two without any silliness, but I like to add an element of fun to everything we do. Simple things like having a Gremlin visit your room overnight can make a difference. It's another layer of fun that makes children want to come to school.

Make It Fun To Clean

I'm an advocate of having the students do most of the cleaning and organizing in the classroom. After all, it's their room, and when they clean it, they acquire a greater sense of ownership and responsibility. I manage the work, but they perform it. And I am careful not to micromanage. I'll give them a task, but then I'll leave them alone and let them decide how to do it.

Again, we make it fun. I'll place a wastepaper basket in the middle of the floor and then lay a strip of masking tape down about ten feet away. When they finish using a paper towel, they'll go to the line and shoot. We make teams and see who makes the most baskets. Every student gets two shots each, and one student's sole responsibility is to manage and officiate this mini game. I know it's simple and silly, but they love it and it makes the work enjoyable.

Breathe Deep

This may sound strange, but a clean and neatly organized room makes me feel good. I can breathe deeper and relax more readily. Think about a time when you walked into a disorganized classroom or a house choked with clutter. How did you feel? Uncomfortable? Nervous? Did it give you the heebie-jeebies? How do people feel when they enter your room? How do your students feel? Does your classroom contribute to the type of learning environment you want for your students?

Three Happy Steps

Try the following three steps and notice how profoundly they will affect your classroom environment. I know you will be pleased.

Step 1 - Throw out or donate any teaching materials you haven't used within the past two years. Take a close look at what's left. Keep only those items that you know you will use, and get rid of the rest. I guarantee you won't miss a thing.

Step 2 - Place an 8 1/2" x 11" plastic bin or basket on the corner of your desk to keep your important papers, and keep the rest of the desk completely clear. During your spare time, address each paper in your basket and then recycle or throw them away. Keep only those papers you can't live without in a folder tucked into a close-at-hand filing cabinet. Stay on top of this routine by spending a few minutes doing this every day. You won't believe how happy seeing your clean and uncluttered desk every morning will make you feel.

> *You won't believe how happy seeing your clean and uncluttered desk every morning will make you feel.*

Step 3 - Have your students clean and organize their desks and the classroom once a week. Assign specific jobs and consider adding an element of fun. Play music, invent a game, or sing a song together. I'm always surprised when I say, "It's Friday and time for us to do our weekly cleaning," and get a cheer from the students.

A Super Timesaver

I'm going to let you in on a secret. I'm almost embarrassed to reveal it. In teaching circles it's verboten to say this, but here it goes: when the students leave for the day, occasionally I have to look for things to do. If I'm caught up on lesson planning and grading, my classroom is so organized that sometimes I don't have anything I *need* to do. I can always find a way to improve a future lesson, but I rarely feel behind, rushed, or overwhelmed. Staying organized and clutter free also happens to be a remarkable timesaver.

A note on the topic of freeing your mind:

It is often said that good teaching requires utilizing the practice of multitasking. I'd like to challenge that belief. The idea of multi-tasking—focusing on more than one thing at a time—is largely a misnomer. The human brain cannot accurately attend to more than one task at a time. Think of talking on the telephone and watching television at the same time. It doesn't work.

A more accurate definition of multitasking is to toggle one's atten-tion from one task to another (or more) and back. As teachers, we sometimes have no choice but to multitask in this manner. Things come up throughout the course of the day that are beyond our con-trol. Research has shown, however, that we (human beings) don't do it very well. Multitasking is proven to waste time, create stress, and cause a loss of focus.

Hence, the more you can concentrate on one thing at a time the bet-ter. Clearing your room of clutter and keeping your desk organized will help immensely, as will many of the keys presented in this book. However, your daily awareness of the ineffectiveness of multitasking will lead you naturally toward ways of limiting its use.

Putting It Into Practice

1. Removing the clutter from your classroom will save vast amounts of time, lower stress, and make you a better teacher.

2. Donate or throw out anything you haven't used within the past two years.

3. Place a small basket in the corner of your desk to keep your important papers, and keep the rest of your desk clear.

4. Set aside a block of time every week for your students to clean their desks and the classroom.

5. Play music, devise games, and make cleaning fun for everyone.

Dream Class

Allow Freedom Within Boundaries

Show Them How

Build Rapport

Give Worthy Praise

Cultivate Independence

Transform Limiting Beliefs

Take Responsibility

Hold Students Accountable

Be A Great Storyteller

Help Shy Students Flourish

Treat The Cause, Not The Symptoms

Involve And Utilize Parents

Develop Maturity

Free Your Room, Free Your Mind

See The Best In Your Students

One Last Thing

I always try to believe
the best of everybody—
it saves so much trouble.

—Rudyard Kipling

Key #15

See The Best In Your Students

Ateacher stopped me one day as I was walking into the school's front office to check my mailbox. He wanted to know about a student of his named Katherine, who I saw earlier in the day as part of an art, science, and P.E. rotation. He asked how well the student was doing and if I found that she had a hard time following directions.

I told the teacher that Katherine was doing well and, for the most part, followed directions just fine. The teacher then began to complain about Katherine and express how frustrated he was with her. It quickly went beyond complaining and escalated into a sharp critique of the student's character.

It's normal for teachers to vent from time to time, but this teacher crossed a line that should never be crossed. I was suddenly uncomfortable participating in the conversation, if only as a listener. Luckily, another teacher walked up and joined in the conversation. I saw my opening and slipped away. As I was leaving the room, I overheard the second teacher say, "I feel so sorry for you. I'm glad I don't have her in my class."

This happened in early December, with many more months left in the school year. I felt badly for Katherine, who would have to endure what was plainly not a good classroom environment for her. I made a mental note to let her know how much I enjoyed having her in my art rotation class. I'm certain that through her teacher's words, actions, and body language, Katherine was well aware of his feelings toward her.

> Too surprised and disgusted to react to her sarcasm, I just nodded my head and walked away.

Twice In One Day

Later that day, our school was hosting an event to raise money for field trips and to build awareness of the many social services available to the community. I was visiting the numerous booths that encircled the playground when I came upon one hosted by a group of teachers. As part of their fundraising efforts, they were offering various tattoos that could be easily washed off with soap and water.

While I was looking at the designs, one of the teachers said, in reference to one of her students, "Gloria asked me if the tattoos were real. Can you believe that? I said to her, 'Yes Gloria, we're selling permanent tattoos.' Hello? How dumb can you get? I was like duh!"

This teacher wasn't whispering or speaking in hushed tones. She was talking freely and loudly in front of other teachers and even in front of a few students and parents. Too surprised to react to her sarcasm, I just nodded my head and walked away.

That evening I was kicking myself for not speaking up and reminding this teacher to be more careful when discussing students. It would have been an awkward conversation, certainly, but also probably the right thing to do. Although we all put our foot in our mouth on occasion, it was clear she needed to reevaluate what her elemental teacher responsibilities were.

Nothing More Than Gossip

Venting to a few close colleagues in private or seeking advice about an unnamed student is one thing, but complaining about or criticizing particular students is improper and unprofessional. A teacher should never discuss a student unless it's positive or part of a professional conversation. To do otherwise is merely gossip, which serves no other purpose than to mollify the frustrations of the speaker and satisfy the desire of the willing listener to (briefly) feel better about his or her own classroom struggles. Tellingly, you will find few exceptional teachers inclined to listen to others gossip or complain about students.

> *A teacher should never discuss a student unless it's positive or part of a professional conversation.*

Protecting Character And Reputation

When parents send a child to school, they are entrusting the teacher with that child's safety and protection. This includes the safety and protection of character and reputation. Talking about students outside of a professional discussion is a betrayal of that trust. It also risks causing lasting harm.

When students hear of fellow classmates gossiping about them, it can be hurtful enough. When the gossip comes from an authority figure like a teacher, it can be especially damaging. Most troubling, those teachers who gossip, complain, or even entertain disparaging thoughts about students are undermining their own success and thus the success of their students.

Your Thoughts About Students Affect Your Teaching

Negative thoughts about students—and the gossip and complaining that spring from them—typically surface as a result of not letting rules and consequences do the job of curbing unwanted behavior. Frustration and helplessness build in reaction to persistently ill-behaved students, and over time these feelings manifest into thoughts of resentment—which will assuredly sabotage your efforts to create a dream class.

> *Whenever you let negative thoughts about students take root in your mind, you'll subconsciously act differently toward them, and they'll know it.*

Have you ever heard the saying, *your thoughts are showing*? Well, it's true. What we spend our time thinking about tends to bubble to the surface in one form or another. Whenever you let negative thoughts about students take root in your mind, you'll subconsciously act differently toward them, and they'll know it. It's something you can't hide. Once this happens, you've lost them and any influence you had with them.

When you verbalize these negative thoughts to others in the form of gossip or complaining, it solidifies your thinking, making it difficult to change. The end result is having to motivate and inspire a number of unhappy students who privately dislike their teacher and are more primed than ever to act out—a sure recipe for failure.

Focusing On Positive Attributes

Negative thinking about students is a habit you must break before you can become a truly effective teacher. Unfortunately, you can't simply decide that you're going to eliminate negative thinking. It doesn't work that way. To be effective, you must replace it with something.

Therefore, when negative thoughts about students begin to creep into your mind, put a stop to them by choosing instead to see only the best in your students. To start, make it a point to be genuinely happy to *all* of them each morning, and try keeping that feeling throughout the day.

> ### The power of positive thinking cannot be underestimated.

Can you convince yourself to be happy to see every student first thing in the morning? Absolutely. The power of positive thinking cannot be underestimated. If you doubt this assertion, try it. Choose a couple of students who offer the greatest challenge to you, and decide for one full week that you're going to like and appreciate them. Focus on their most positive attributes, and when you greet them in the morning, tell them you're happy to see them.

After this one-week experiment, I'm certain that you will begin to see your students in a different light. The greatest benefit of changing your thinking habits, however, is that you will notice an unmistakable but delightful change in the way your students react to you. Keep it up for a month, and you'll wonder why you ever had an unconstructive thought about them in the first place.

Another benefit is that you will no longer feel the self-defeating need to air your frustrations to other teachers or to listen to them complain about their own students.

The old adage that you should avoid the teachers' lounge is a good one. There is no reason to subject yourself to negative confabulation or risk polluting your positive attitude. It's better to avoid the temptation of joining the "whine and cheese" parties altogether, and eat lunch with only like-minded colleagues.

Stop Arguing, Demanding, Negotiating, And Pleading

If there are students who are not measuring up to the expectations you have for your class, then let them know and hold them accountable. Be straight with them and tell them where they've gone wrong, but don't take their behavior personally. Simply and calmly deliver your predetermined consequences, and stop arguing, demanding, negotiating, and pleading with them. These ineffectual methods will only lead to your frustration and more and more of the same unwanted behaviors.

Professional Settings Only

No student has the right to disrupt your class, but they do have the right to have their transgressions handled professionally. Parents, counselors, administrators, and occasionally other teachers may need to be informed of a child's behavior in a professional setting. All other settings are off limits. The trust you are given by parents for six hours each day seals an unspoken contract between you.

When parents send their children off to school, it's with the assumption that you will treat them with respect and dignity. When you gossip or complain about them, you break that contract and, at the same time, damage your hope of creating a dream class.

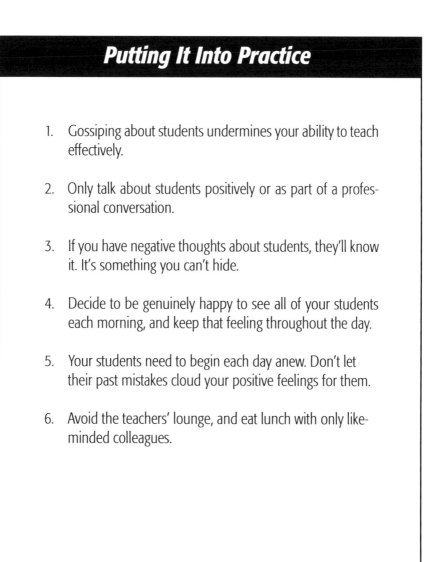

Putting It Into Practice

1. Gossiping about students undermines your ability to teach effectively.

2. Only talk about students positively or as part of a professional conversation.

3. If you have negative thoughts about students, they'll know it. It's something you can't hide.

4. Decide to be genuinely happy to see all of your students each morning, and keep that feeling throughout the day.

5. Your students need to begin each day anew. Don't let their past mistakes cloud your positive feelings for them.

6. Avoid the teachers' lounge, and eat lunch with only like-minded colleagues.

Dream Class

Allow Freedom Within Boundaries

Show Them How

Build Rapport

Give Worthy Praise

Cultivate Independence

Transform Limiting Beliefs

Take Responsibility

Hold Students Accountable

Be A Great Storyteller

Help Shy Students Flourish

Treat The Cause, Not The Symptoms

Involve And Utilize Parents

Develop Maturity

Free Your Room, Free Your Mind

See The Best In Your Students

One Last Thing

Nothing exhilarates and sends the soul soaring more than having a good time—so much so that face muscles ache from such hearty laughter.

—Sister Karol Jackowski

One Last Thing

I'm often asked a variation of the same question. It comes from parents as well as other teachers:

"What are you doing that makes your students enjoy being in your classroom so much?"

The answer is reflected in the previous 15 chapters. Creating your dream class and becoming an exceptional teacher includes not only your happiness and fulfillment, but also that of your students. By following the previous 15 keys, your students will love being part of your class. Of that, I have complete confidence. However, there is something I didn't include but has always been a significant part of my teaching: humor.

If you have used humor in the past, then you know what a positive effect it can have on students. If they love your class after using the 15 keys—and they will—using humor will put them over the top.

Keep in mind, if your students admire you and love being in your class, you have powerful leverage and influence, making everything you do as a teacher infinitely easier and more effective.

Influencing Difficult Students

Humor is a teacher's secret weapon. It's secret because few teachers use humor purposely. I began using humor my first day of teaching because it made teaching more fun. It wasn't long, however, before I realized it was a useful tool in reaching even the most difficult students. When I think of the most challenging students I've had over the years, I can often credit humor as an important factor in influencing them.

> *Humor is a teacher's secret weapon.*

Why Isn't Humor One Of The 15 Keys?

I was reluctant to include the use of humor as one of the 15 keys for three reasons. First, I don't believe using humor is essential in creating your dream class. It's important that you are friendly and approachable, but I don't think it's critical that you be able make your students laugh.

Second, it's not for everyone. We all have different personalities, and not every teacher feels comfortable using humor in the classroom. I know teachers who create wonderful learning environments and have happy and motivated students, who don't use humor.

Third, I was concerned about being misunderstood. I like to have fun and laugh a lot with my students, but my primary objective is that they become tenacious learners and responsible people. Humor must never interfere with this goal. If you're inclined, however, there is a place for it in your classroom.

How To Use Humor

You don't have to be a comedian to use humor. All it takes is a little creativity and a lack of self-consciousness. Your students will appreciate any attempt at humor. When I loan a pencil to a student, I can't resist saying to them, "Please take care of it. My grandma gave me this pencil for my birthday, and it means a lot to me." They rarely laugh out loud, and I know it's not sidesplitting funny, but little amusements like this throughout the day can make a difference.

Another question I'm often asked is:

"What exactly do you do to incorporate humor into your teaching? Give me some examples."

> *When I tell a joke, you can hear crickets chirping after I deliver the punch line.*

This is a tough question to answer because humor doesn't always translate from one person to another. We all have unique personalities and humor preferences. The humor I use in my classroom may not be your style, or even work for you.

For example, my friend Jim is a great joke teller. Regardless of the joke, when he tells it, it's funny and everyone laughs. When I tell a joke, you can hear crickets chirping after I deliver the punch line. It just doesn't work for me. When using humor in your classroom, it's important to be yourself and go with what works for you.

Examples

I understand, however, the need to know what has worked in the past. So in this spirit—and against my will—here are a few examples of things I do to make my students laugh.

♦If I notice a chair left out—maybe the offending student went to sharpen a pencil or get some paper—I'll pretend to trip over it. I'll throw papers in the air and get tangled in the chair as I go down. As the kids are helping me up, I'll look around dazed with my eyes crossed and say, "What happened? The last thing I remember, I was walking by Jose's desk."

◆Many times I've pretended that I was someone else. I'll put on a wig and wear clothes I don't normally wear and present myself as the substitute teacher for the day. I'll usually be a surfer dude, but I've also been a robot and my own twin brother. I'll stay in character for 20 minutes or so and then go back to being Mr. Linsin.

> *"If it happens again, we're going to hang you upside down from the ceiling fan and throw tomatoes at you."*

◆If a student is sharing a long-drawn-out answer, I'll lie down on the floor and pretend to go to sleep.

◆If a student unintentionally breaks a simple class rule, like continuing to work when I'm giving instructions, I'll say, "Daisy, please give me your attention. You have a warning. If it happens again, we're going to hang you upside down from the ceiling fan and throw tomatoes at you."

◆Sometimes I'll give directions using a funny accent—British, Irish, and Jamaican are my favorites. I also do—or try to do—Rocky Balboa, Dracula, Yoda, Shaggy (from Scooby Doo), and a military commander. Are my impressions any good? No. They're probably terrible, and I would never consider doing them in front of adults, but my students *love* them and think they're funny.

◆I make up silly nicknames for each student. I'll use them once a week or so to release students to recess. To give you an example, I got out a phone book and randomly (honest) selected three names: Bill Foto, Jill Griffin, and Jonathon Paslov. Here is what I would call them if they were in my class: Bill "will you take my" Foto, Jill Gryffendor (from Harry Potter), and Jonathon Paslov's dog. Most students love nicknames, but not all students. Beforehand, I'll ask if there is anyone who doesn't want to be called a nickname, and I oblige.

◆Occasionally, when I have to give simple procedural directions, I'll sing them like an opera singer. My students will ask questions back the same way, singing, "Whaaaat haaaapennnns if I fooorget my backpaaaaack?" I'll answer, "Then youuuuuu will beeee in big troubllllllllllllle." Everybody laughs at this one.

◆When going to the library on campus, we'll pretend we're ninja warriors planning an attack on an evil fortress. Instead of walking in a boring line, we'll sneak our way across campus, lightly tiptoeing from tree to tree, hiding behind bushes and corners. I'm always the lead ninja, and I play the part to the hilt. I'll teach them a few hand signals—get down, proceed with caution, someone's approaching, target in sight. We'll duck when we sneak by rooms and make a game of not being detected. Other teachers look at me like I'm nuts, but it's a blast! The students smile and laugh the whole way. When we arrive at the library, it's business as usual.

Humor Is Everywhere

Opportunities like these to have fun and laugh are everywhere if you look. Use your imagination. Ideas that come from you are best. If you find it difficult bringing humor to your classroom, think of close family members. Nothing brings out humor more than the intimacy of family. Rarely seen by others, the little moments of silliness and laughter you share with loved ones is precious. Try bringing that same feeling of relaxed humor to your classroom, and you may find that it softens even the most challenging students.

Putting It Into Practice

1. Humor can help you gain more influence with your students, making everything you do as a teacher infinitely easier and more effective.

2. Humor is a useful tool in reaching even the most difficult students.

3. Anyone can add a little humor to the classroom. All it takes is a little creativity and a lack of self-consciousness.

4. Your students will appreciate any attempt at humor.

5. Be yourself. Ideas that come from you are best.

Dream Class

Preface

Postscript

May your strength give us strength
May your faith give us faith
May your hope give us hope
May your love give us love

—Bruce Springsteen, "Into The Fire"

Postscript

Driving to work on the freeway one rainy morning, I glanced into my rearview mirror and noticed a car approaching too quickly behind me. When it got closer, I recognized the driver as a coworker. Due to the slick roads, I was driving less than the 65-mile-per-hour speed limit. I had just moved into one of two exit lanes that run about a mile in length before the impending exit.

This colleague of mine continued to accelerate frighteningly close to my bumper. At first I thought he must have recognized me and was trying to get my attention, but one look at his frustrated expression told me otherwise. He rode my bumper into the exit, and when he saw an opening, he roared around me.

Now driving on a typical city road, he zigzagged ahead of me and turned left a half mile in the distance and onto a road I wasn't familiar with. I assumed he had found a shortcut or that maybe he was trying to pretend he wasn't who I thought he was.

When I got to the corner nearest the school, I turned right and then began turning left into the driveway and through the entrance to the parking lot. As I did, I saw him pull in front of me from the opposite direction. Our eyes met and his face whitened with mortification.

I knew his behavior on the freeway was nothing personal. It was clear he hadn't recognized me. But knowing this did little to calm my now frayed and tattered nerves.

I never want to be in this state of mind when I teach. Despite my colleague's aggressive driving and my stressed reaction to it, I had a job to do. It's one of the most difficult aspects of teaching; you always have to be on, regardless of whether you're feeling ill or upset or annoyed because a colleague cut you off.

I took some deep breaths and tried to calm myself before greeting my students. I paced about my classroom, brooding, waiting for the seconds to tick down and the bell to ring for the start of school. The sun was just beginning to peek out from behind the scattering storm clouds when the bell rang.

As I stepped out of the classroom, I had every intention of putting the driving incident behind me, but it wasn't working. I was still on edge as I approached a set of stairs that led to the playground where I was to meet my class.

I bounded up the stairs two at a time determined to put on a good face for my students. When I got to the top, I could see them about 20 paces ahead. They were all smiles and goofiness, happily chatting away. A few of them nearest the front spotted me and shushed and jostled the others into a straight line.

When I reached them, I took a quick inventory of who was there while they stared back at me, still smiling and now excited to begin the day. As I was counting them, I involuntarily began smiling back. They had their faces upturned toward me, attentive and happy, anticipating another fun day of learning. This was my dream class.

In spite of myself, I let out a small chuckle and then broke into a wide grin, mirroring their expressions. Before turning to lead them to the classroom, I exhaled for what seemed like the first time that day, and the problems of the morning dissipated with the breaking clouds.

My hope is for you to create your own dream class, one that does as much for you as you do for them. Regardless of where you teach or who your students are, it's within your grasp. Apply each of the 15 keys earnestly and consistently, and you will soon begin to see your class transforming into the one you dreamed of when you first decided to become a teacher.

Note:

If, after reading *Dream Class,* you feel in any way overwhelmed by the number of changes you'd like to make to your classroom...well, there is no reason to be. I've made every mistake in this and any other book—some ten times over. You can do it. I promise. And I'm not going to leave you on your own.

Head on over to smartclassroommanagement.com and sign up for our free newsletter. Week after week you'll receive simple-to-use tips, solutions, and strategies to help you put all 15 keys, and much more, into action.

See you there!

-Michael

Made in the USA
Las Vegas, NV
14 January 2022

41353967R00109